JUMPS
PSH

C000256900

This collection of engaging and simple to use activities will jumpstart students' understanding of themselves and their relationships, and their knowledge of how to lead a healthy lifestyle.

A wealth of practical activities in the book range from class and group discussions and formal debates to games, role plays, hotseating and thought tracking. This book enables teachers to deliver effective and imaginative PSHE lessons, encouraging children to:

- share their views on issues that concern them such as bullying;
- learn to think for themselves and to make their own decisions;
- be aware of the dangers involved in drinking, smoking and drug-taking;
- understand their relationships with family and friends;
- explore social issues such as prejudice and discrimination;
- learn how to handle their emotions.

Jumpstart! PSHE is an essential classroom resource that will encourage the personal development of children and is the perfect tool to help teachers deliver effective and imaginative PSHE lessons.

John Foster taught English for 20 years before becoming a full-time writer. He has written over 100 books for classroom use and is a highly regarded children's poet.

Jumpstart!

Jumpstart! PSHE
Games and activities for ages 7–13
John Foster

Jumpstart! History
Engaging activities for ages 7–12
Sarah Whitehouse and Karan Vickers-Hulse

Jumpstart! Geography
Engaging activities for ages 7–12
Mark Jones and Sarah Whitehouse

Jumpstart! Thinking Skills and Problem Solving
Games and activities for ages 7–14
Steve Bowkett

Jumpstart! Maths (2nd Edition)
Maths activities and games for ages 5–14
John Taylor

Jumpstart! Grammar
Games and activities for ages 7–14
Pie Corbett and Julia Strong

Jumpstart! Spanish and Italian
Engaging activities for ages 7–12
Catherine Watts and Hilary Phillips

Jumpstart! French and German
Engaging activities for ages 7–12
Catherine Watts and Hilary Phillips

Jumpstart! Drama
Games and activities for ages 5–11
Teresa Cremin, Roger McDonald, Emma Goff and Louise Blakemore

Jumpstart! Science
Games and activities for ages 5–11
Rosemary Feasey

Jumpstart! Storymaking
Games and activities for ages 7–12
Pie Corbett

Jumpstart! Poetry
Games and activities for ages 7–12
Pie Corbett

Jumpstart! Creativity
Games and activities for ages 7–14
Steve Bowkett

Jumpstart! ICT
ICT activities and games for ages 7–14
John Taylor

Jumpstart! Numeracy
Maths activities and games for ages 5–14
John Taylor

Jumpstart! Literacy
Key Stage 2/3 literacy games
Pie Corbett

JUMPSTART!
PSHE

GAMES AND ACTIVITIES FOR AGES 7–13

John Foster

Routledge
Taylor & Francis Group

LONDON AND NEW YORK

First published 2015
by Routledge
2 Park Square, Milton Park, Abingdon, Oxon OX14 4RN

and by Routledge
711 Third Avenue, New York, NY 10017

Routledge is an imprint of the Taylor & Francis Group, an informa business

British Library Cataloguing in Publication Data
A catalogue record for this book is available from the British Library

Library of Congress Cataloging in Publication Data
Foster, John, 1941 October 12–
Jumpstart! PSHE : games and activities for ages 7-13 / John Foster.
pages cm
1. Social skills--Study and teaching (Elementary)--Activity programs. 2. Social
skills—Study and teaching (Middle)—Activity programs. 3. Life skills—Study
and teaching (Middle)—Activity programs. 4. Life skills—Study and teaching
(Middle)—Activity programs. I. Title.
LB1139.S6F67 2015
302'.14—dc23
2014043141

ISBN: 978-1-138-89220-0 (hbk)
ISBN: 978-1-138-89221-7 (pbk)
ISBN: 978-1-315-70922-2 (ebk)

Typeset in Palatino and Scala Sans
by FiSH Books Ltd, Enfield

Printed and bound in Great Britain by
TJ International Ltd, Padstow, Cornwall

Contents

Contents

Acknowledgements

The following poems:

'Market forces', 'The recycling rap', 'Modified progress', 'Where is the forest?', 'It isn't right to fight', 'Moving on', 'The vase', 'I was bullied once', 'And how was school today?', 'My little sister', 'Why did you pull her hair?', 'Great-gran just sits' – © John Foster 2007 from *The Poetry Chest* (Oxford University Press).

'Victor the vandal' © John Foster 2015.

Introduction

Although Personal, Social and Health Education is not a statutory requirement, and there are, therefore, no National Curriculum programmes of study for PSHE, all schools are expected to include it as part of their wider curriculum. It is an important part of all pupils' education and it is up to schools to tailor their PSHE programme to the needs of their pupils, equipping them with the knowledge and skills to make safe and informed decisions in their lives.

In primary schools, most teachers, whatever their subject specialism, find themselves in the position of having to teach PSHE lessons to their class and in many secondary schools non-specialists are required, as part of their role as form tutors, to deliver PSHE lessons to their forms. The aim of *Jumpstart! PSHE* is to provide straightforward, easy-to-use activities that the teacher responsible for co-ordinating PSHE can integrate into the school's programme and that will enable the class teacher or form tutor to deliver effective lessons that the children will find interesting and informative.

Jumpstart! PSHE is arranged in three parts, according to the themes which form the core of PSHE programmes in both primary and secondary schools: developing self-knowledge and understanding relationships, keeping healthy and living in the wider world.

Within the section on self-knowledge and understanding relationships there are units on handling emotions and developing self-esteem and on managing time and money, as well as on relationships with family and friends. Within the keeping healthy section there are units on healthy eating, the importance of exercise and on drinking, smoking and illegal drugs, as well as on puberty, contraception and safer sex. Living in the wider world contains units on values and beliefs, human rights, stereotyping and discrimination, rules and responsibilities and on the environment and global issues such as world health and world hunger. The aim is to provide stimulating activities that can be used either as starters when introducing a new topic or that will fit alongside the other materials being used during a topic rather than to provide a comprehensive coverage of the topic.

Activities range from formal debates and discussions, ranking exercises and quizzes to games, role play and hotseating. Many of the activities involve the children in groups or pairs discussing issues and sharing opinions, thus providing individuals with an opportunity to consider various viewpoints and develop their own ideas.

SETTING GROUND RULES

It is important to set ground rules for class and group discussions in order to ensure that the children respect each other's feelings and views and that the discussion remains focused and is conducted in an orderly way. A good way of doing this is to involve the children themselves in setting the ground rules. This can be done as a circle time activity with a class of younger juniors or as a group discussion activity, with an older junior class or a lower secondary form.

Ask the younger children in their circle to say what they think helps a group work well together. List the points the class makes on a large sheet of paper, which can be put on the wall as a reminder that can be referred to whenever you ask them to have a group discussion. The points made by the groups of older children can similarly be displayed. The guidelines should include such things as listening to and respecting what other people say, taking turns and not interrupting, sticking to the task, not putting pressure on others to reveal things they would rather not talk about and encouraging everyone in the group to participate.

In order to ensure that a group discussion is conducted in an orderly fashion, it is a good idea to appoint one of the children to act as a chairperson to say whose turn it is to speak and to keep the group on task. With older children, it is also worth getting one of the group to act as secretary and to make notes of the different views that are expressed. Alternatively, they can choose someone to act as reporter and to report the group's views to the rest of the class.

When discussing issues in groups, it is important for the children to realise that they do not always have to reach a decision with which everyone agrees. Often, when reporting a group's views to the class, it is necessary for the reporter to say that the group's opinions were divided.

ROLE PLAY

Throughout the book there are a number of suggestions for role plays varying from those in which the children are asked to take on the roles of a number of characters e.g. in a public meeting to scenarios involving two people, such as interviews, discussions between friends or between an adult and a child. Often it is a good idea to ask the children to perform a role play twice so that they get the opportunity to experience both sides of an argument.

The value of role plays is that they help the children to explore different points of view and to empathise with different characters. When asking pairs to perform, you can either get the whole class to perform their role plays simultaneously or choose one pair at a time to perform before the whole class. Which method you use may depend on what space is available.

When the children are performing role plays, it is helpful before they begin to give them a short period of time in which to think themselves into their characters. You can ask the children to adopt a starting position and to freeze that position for a few seconds before you tell them they can start.

Allow time for discussion afterwards in which the participants can reflect on the thoughts and feelings of the characters and answer any questions about why they showed the characters behaving as they did.

The aim of this book is to provide activities that will involve the children, because they deal with issues that are relevant to their lives in an interesting and informative way. Teachers will find the activities useful in delivering PSHE lessons that are enjoyable as well as educational.

PART 1

Developing self-knowledge and understanding relationships

CHAPTER 1
Understanding yourself

This chapter aims to provide activities that will help children to recognise their strengths, to consider what they are good at and what their interests are and to identify positive features of their personality. It also contains activities to encourage them to think about the future, identifying their priorities, discussing attitudes to work and what it means to be an adult.

HOW DO YOU DO? (Year 3 circle activity)

Aim: To help the children to begin to understand their own strengths and those of other people.

This is an introductory activity in which the children move round the circle shaking hands with each other and introducing themselves by saying, 'How do you do? I'm...' and telling each other their name, one thing they are good at, one thing that they hope to become better at during year 3.

WE'VE GOT TALENT (Years 3 and 4 circle activity)

Aim: To recognise what each individual is good at and that everyone has different talents.

In circle time, get them to talk about their hobbies and what they like doing. Encourage them to think about things that they are good at doing. Then tell them to write down on separate pieces of paper one thing that they like doing and one thing that they are good at. Place a box labelled 'Our Talent Box' in the middle of the room and get them to put their pieces of paper in it anonymously.

Conclude the session by picking some of the pieces of paper out of the box and getting the class to guess who wrote them.

As a follow-up, you can invite the children to take turns in the following weeks to prepare a short talk about their hobby to give to the class. At the end of each talk encourage the children to ask questions about the person's hobby.

IF (Years 3 and 4 circle activity)

Aim: To get the children thinking about themselves and their lives.

In this activity you go round the circle asking the children first to talk about their likes and dislikes, then about what changes they'd make in their lives if they could. Tell them that they do not have to say anything when it's their turn, if they'd prefer not to do so, and just to say 'Pass'.

Round 1   One thing I like doing in my spare time.
Round 2   One thing I like doing at school.
Round 3   One thing I hate.
Round 4   One thing I'd like to change at home.
Round 5   One thing I'd like to change at school.
Round 6   One thing I'd like to change about myself.

End the session by talking about some of the things they suggested changing. Discuss how easy or difficult it would be to make the changes.

WHAT SORT OF PERSON ARE YOU? (Years 5 and 6 card game)

Aim: To encourage each of the children to recognise positive aspects of their personality.

This is a game for groups of four. Ask the children to make a set of cards for their group with the following character traits written on separate cards:

3

shy, confident, kind, cheerful, ambitious, honest, reliable, polite, truthful, dependable, thoughtful, sympathetic, open to advice, tolerant, generous, supportive, even-tempered, helpful, patient, decisive, caring, well-behaved, hard-working, considerate, friendly, adventurous, brave, open to criticism, sensitive, trustworthy.

Explain that the object of the game is for each of them to collect three cards with characteristics which they think apply to them. They shuffle the cards and they take turns to draw a card from the pack. If they think the card describes one of their strengths they keep it. If they think it doesn't, they return it to the bottom of the pack. The game continues until all four of them have three cards. They then show the three cards to the other members of the group who challenge them to give a reason why they think the card applies to them. For example, when challenged to explain why they choose to keep the card saying kind, one of them might say, 'I think I am kind because...' and quote an incident in which they showed kindness.

WHAT ARE YOUR STRENGTHS? (Years 5 and 6 card game)

Aim: To help the children to identify strengths.

This is a game for groups of three children. Ask the children to make a set of cards for their group with the following skills written on separate cards:

good listener, can explain ideas, can give reasons for views, can negotiate, can follow instructions, good at problem-solving, well-organised, good at making things, can express opinions orally, can identify key points, good at researching, can express views in writing.

Shuffle the cards and take turns to pick a card. The children must decide whether or not they have that skill. If they think they have that skill, they must show the card to the other two players and give their reasons for saying that they have the skill. If they cannot convince the other two players, the card is returned to the bottom of the pack. Once one person has three cards, they are the winner.

The other two continue to play until one of them gets to keep three cards. The third member of the group plays on until they too have three cards.

THE FUTURE I'D LIKE (Years 5–8 discussion)

Aim: To get the children think about what their priorities are.

Ask the children to think about what their life would be like in an ideal world in the future and to write down what they would like to have done by the age of 25. Ask them to think of up to five things they would like to have done. Prompt them to think about such things as go to university, own my own house, travel round the world, play in a pop group, make a lot of money, have a job that helps people, get married, have children, play for England, climb Mount Everest, own a fast car, own my own business.

Encourage them to share their ideas with a partner and to discuss how their ideas are different and what this tells each of them about what their priorities are and what is important to them.

WHAT IS WORK? (Years 6 and 7 making a collage)

Aim: To understand that there are different kinds of work.

Ask the children: What do we mean by work? Give groups copies of old newspapers and magazines and invite them to make a collage which illustrates the different kinds of work that people do. Prompt them to think about such things as physical work and mental work, paid work and voluntary work, manual workers and clerical workers. Encourage them to include words from job adverts as well as pictures in their collages. When they have completed their collages, ask them to show them to the other groups and to explain why they have included the pictures and words that they have.

WHAT SORT OF JOB DO YOU WANT? (Years 6 and 7 ranking activity)

Aim: To discuss their attitudes to different types of jobs.

Ask the children: What sort of job interests them? Do they want a job simply to earn money or because it will help people? Do you want a job that will give you status? What is most important to them? Put the list of types of job (below) on the board and ask them to rank each one according to how important it is to them on a scale of 1 to 10 in which 10 is very important and 1 is not important. Encourage them to compare their scores with a partner and to discuss what their scores reveal about their attitudes to work.

- A job that helps people
- A job that gives me status
- A job that's not boring
- A job that I can get promoted in
- A job that doesn't require lots of exams
- A job that involves working with people
- An indoor job
- An outdoor job
- A well-paid job
- A job that interests me and gives job satisfaction
- A job without too much responsibility
- A job that enables me to make full use of my skills.

BECOMING AN ADULT (Years 7–8 discussion)

Aim: To consider what being an adult means.

Ask the children individually to write down what they think being an adult means. Collect their ideas on the board and discuss what being grown up means. Guide the discussion so that you get them to think about such things as acting responsibly, making your own decisions, tolerating and respecting other people's beliefs and opinions, being reliable and keeping promises. Ask pairs to divide a sheet of paper into two columns labelled 'Childish behaviour' and 'Adult behaviour' and to list examples of each. For example, under Childish behaviour' they might put 'Sulking when you don't get your own way' and under adult behaviour 'Accepting that you can't get your own way all the time'.

CHAPTER 2
Family matters

The aim of this chapter is to explore the different types of families there are and how the members of families care for and share with one another. There are activities which examine relationships within families and situations in which quarrels and arguments occur between parents and children over such things as who does the chores and who makes decisions. Other activities focus on living with brothers and sisters and on having an elderly relative living with the family.

WHAT IS A FAMILY? (Years 3 and 4 discussion/drawing a family tree)

Aim: To understand that there are different types of family.

Introduce the topic by explaining that there are several different types of family.

Ask groups 'What is a family? What different types of family are there? Share their ideas in a class discussion and write them on the board. Point out that there are many different types of family – one-parent families, childless couples, step-families, families in which there are adopted children and foster families. Mention that families vary in size from two people to large families with lots of relatives.

Explain what a family tree is and as an example draw up a family tree of the Royal family. Talk about how each person on the family tree is related to the others in the Royal family. Discuss how some people can draw detailed family trees, whereas other people know very little about their relatives.

Encourage those of them who can do so to bring in photos of their relatives and to show them to the class and talk about the different relatives people have: parents, brothers and sisters, grandparents, uncles and aunts and cousins.

SHARING AND CARING (Years 3 and 4 discussion/writing)

Aim: To investigate how different members of the family help each other.

Ask groups: How do members of a family help each other? Get them to make a list of all the things that people living together do for one another. Prompt them as necessary to include such things as shopping for food and clothes, cleaning, tidying, washing, putting out the rubbish, looking after the baby, paying bills, doing the garden. Then, make a list of all the members of the family or adults that they live with and talk about who does what.

Ask: Are any of the jobs always done by the same person? Which person in the family does the most to help the rest of the family?

Conclude the activity by asking the children to think of one thing on their lists that they could take responsibility for doing.

THE VASE (Years 3 and 4 a poem to discuss)

Aim: To discuss what to do in a situation in which a family member is upset.

Read the poem 'The Vase' and discuss what the children are feeling as they wait for the mother to arrive. Ask them: What will the mother feel when she realises they have broken the vase? Will it make a difference if one of the children responsible is a friend rather than a brother or sister?

The vase

We've picked up all the pieces.
We've brushed and swept the floor.
We're waiting, listening for the click
Of Mum's key in the door.

We're wondering how to tell her.
We're wondering how to say
We broke the vase her Grandma gave her
On her wedding day.

Encourage the children to share their own experiences of similar situations in which they have broken or damaged something of sentimental value to their parents or have done something that really upset their parents.

Invite groups of three to role play the scene in which the children tell the mother that they have broken the vase. Encourage them to discuss how the vase came to be broken and to think about how the mother might react differently depending on how the accident happened.

LIVING WITH BROTHERS AND SISTERS (Years 5 and 6 discussion/role play/writing)

Aim: To discuss relationships with brothers and sisters.

Ask the class to think about what it is like being in a family with brothers or sisters or about being an only child. Get them to write down one thing they like about having a brother or a sister or being an only child and one thing they dislike.

Then hold a class discussion. Ask: What are the good things about having a brother or a sister? What games or activities do you do together? What annoys you about your brother or sister? When do you get angry with each other? What would you miss if you didn't have a brother or sister? What are the good things about being an only child?

On the board list the advantages and disadvantages of having brothers or sisters.

Focus on arguments between brothers and sisters. Talk about situations in which brothers and sisters quarrel. Invite them to role play one or more of the following situations:

- An argument because they want to watch different programmes on the TV.
- A quarrel because one of them borrowed something without permission.
- An argument because one of them won't take turns playing with something.
- A quarrel because one of them tries to blame the other for breaking or damaging something.

Before they begin, tell them that instead of letting the argument go on for ever, they must work out an ending for the situation. Brainstorm alternative endings that the situations might have – for example, one of them might give way, one of them might stalk off in a temper, one of them might admit they were in the wrong and apologise, the two of them might agree a compromise.

Ask some of them to present their role plays to the rest of the class. Discuss which of their role plays show the situation being resolved in the most productive way.

As a follow-up activity, the children can write a script about a situation in which sisters or brothers quarrel or an only child quarrels with a cousin. They could introduce a parent to settle the dispute – either fairly or unfairly. They can then read their scripts to the class.

End the work on brothers and sisters positively by discussing situations in which brothers and sisters can support and help each other. They can share problems and worries, for example, if their parents are planning to separate or if they are worried because one of their parents has lost their job. They may be able to offer support and advice if you are being bullied or teased, or one of your friends no longer wants to be a friend. They can help and support each other, for example when their brother or sister is sad, unhappy or ill.

A FAMILY CODE OF BEHAVIOUR (Years 5 and 6 discussion/ writing)

Aim: To draw up a family code of behaviour.

Ask groups to discuss what kinds of behaviour help family members to get on well with each other. Invite them to draw up a list of rules for family members to follow that will help them to live happily with each other. Prompt them to include rules about sharing and caring, understanding others' feelings and respecting their privacy and their property, and about treating other family members as you like them to treat you.

Encourage them to compare their code of behaviour with the codes of behaviour drawn up by other groups and get them to add any suggestions that other groups make which they think are worth including in their lists of rules.

WHO DECIDES? (Years 7 and 8 discussion)

Aim: To discuss who makes decisions about your life and how old you need to be before you make your own decisions.

Talk about how parents or guardians make decisions for young children about matters such as what clothes they wear and where they can go when they go out to play. Explain that, as children grow up, they gradually take responsibility for making their own decisions.

Put this list on the board and ask the children individually to write down whether they think the decision should be made by a child or their parent(s)/guardians. Say at what age you think a person is old enough to make the decision themselves.

- How late you can stay out
- How much pocket money you get
- Whether you can sleep over at a friend's house
- What clothes you wear
- What foods you eat
- What school you go to
- What computer sites you can visit
- What videos and TV programmes you watch
- What hairstyle you have
- What make up and jewellery you can wear
- What friends you have
- What music you listen to
- When you do your homework
- What household task you do
- How your room is decorated
- What clubs you can join
- Where you go for a family holiday
- How you spend your money.

WHOSE CHORES? (Years 5–8 discussion)

Aim: To discuss household tasks and who should do them.

Ask the children in groups to make a list of what tasks need to be done at home. Their lists should include: making and changing your bed, tidying your room, cleaning other rooms, cooking meals., setting the table, clearing dishes and washing up, shopping for food, washing clothes, ironing, tidying the garden, cleaning the car, cleaning out/feeding pets, looking after your bicycle, putting games away.

Then ask the children to discuss each of the tasks and to decide whose responsibility it should be to do the task. Ask them to put A for adult beside those tasks for which they think an adult should be responsible, C beside those for which a child should take responsibility and A/C for tasks which should be shared.

Finally, share their views in a class discussion.

THE LADDER OF RESPONSIBILITY (Years 7 and 8 game for groups of four or six)

Aim: To discuss the importance of taking on responsibilities.

This is a game that groups can play which teaches them the importance of taking responsibility. Divide the class into groups of four or six and ask the children in pairs or threes to draw a rope ladder on a large sheet of paper with steps from 1 to 25. Give each of them a counter to place on step 1 and two dice which they take it in turns to roll. Put the questions (below) on the board. Then ask the children to take turns rolling the two dice. The number they roll is the number of the question they must answer. Explain that they should answer truthfully. If they answer yes, they move the counter 4 steps up the ladder. If they answer sometimes they move the counter 2 steps up the ladder. If they answer no, the counter remains where it is. The winner is the person who reaches the top of the ladder first.

At the end of the game ask the children what the game teaches them about taking responsibility for helping others and doing things for themselves. If they answered no to any of the questions, invite them to suggest what they could do in the future to take more responsibility.

2   Do you always hang up your clothes and put dirty clothes in the washing basket?

3   Do you apologise if you have behaved badly?

4   Do you offer to help others without being told to do so?

5   Do you clear away your dishes at the end of a meal?

6   Do you rely on others to make sure you are ready for school on time?

7   Can you be trusted to keep appointments you have arranged?

8   Do you always own up if it's your fault?

9   Do you do regular chores to help the adults at home?

10   Do you ever prepare your own meals?

11   Do you do your homework without having to be told to do it?

12   Do you put away games after you have finished playing them?

ARGUMENTS AND QUARRELS (Years 7 and 8 role play)

Aim: To explore what causes conflict between parents and children and ways of resolving arguments.

Discuss with the class what causes arguments between parents and children, and make a list on the board of the various issues which cause arguments. Then invite the children in pairs to role play the following situations.

- *'You are not to go round there again.'*

A scene in which a parent and a child have an argument because the parent does not like the friends the child has been playing with.

- *'Why can't I go? Everyone else is allowed to go.'*

A scene in which a parent won't allow the child to do something that they desperately want to do.

- *'I can't wear this. Everyone will laugh at me.'*

A scene in which a parent and a child argue over an item of clothing which the parent insists on buying for the child to wear.

Encourage the children to do the role play at least twice with the outcome being different. In one instance, show the child being left feeling resentful and not convinced by the parent's arguments. In the other instance, show the parent and child reaching some kind of agreement that defuses the situation.

PROBLEMS WITH PARENTS (Years 7 and 8 radio phone-in)

Aim: To discuss advice on how to deal with problems with parents.

Invite the children to take it in turns to be the presenter of a radio phone-in programme in which children phone in to ask advice about problems they are having with the adult(s) they live with. The class can either think of problems themselves or use the ones listed below.

'My mum has split up with my dad and I live with my mum. I'm supposed to see my dad every other weekend, but my mum often makes up a reason why I can't see him. I want to see my dad. What can I do?'

'My problem is I don't get on with my step-dad. He's much stricter than my dad used to be and he treats me differently from the way he treats his own two children. It's not fair.'

'I'm not allowed to do lots of the things my friends are allowed to do. I have to stop playing and go in long before they do and my parents won't let me go into town with them. And they won't let me play the computer games my friends play, because they say they are too violent.'

LIVING WITH OTHER RELATIVES (Years 5–8 discussion)

Aim: To explore what it is like having relatives living with you.

Use the poem 'Great-gran just sits' to introduce a discussion of what it can be like to have an elderly relative living with you. Explain what a stroke is and that Great-gran has had a stroke and that she has dementia.

Talk about what life is like for Great-gran and how giving someone like her the care she needs can affect the life of the person who is her carer. Encourage them to share their experiences of having an elderly relative come to live with them. Ask: What difference can having an elderly relative to live with you make to your family life?

Great-gran just sits

Great-gran just sits
All day long there,
Beside the fire,
Propped in her chair.

Sometimes she mumbles
Or gives a shout,
But we can't tell
What it's about.

Great-gran just sits
All day long there.
Her face is blank,
An empty stare.

When anyone speaks,
What does she hear?
When Great-gran shakes
What does she fear?

Great-gran just sits,
Almost alone,
In some dream world
All of her own.

But when Mum bends
Tucking her rug
Perhaps she senses
That loving hug.

CHAPTER 3
Friends and friendships

This chapter consists of activities that explore the qualities that a good friend has and that encourage the children to discuss what to do in situations in which they encounter problems with friends. There is also an activity for older children focusing on what is acceptable and unacceptable in close friendships.

HAVE YOU SEEN MY FRIEND? (Years 3 and 4 circle game)

Aim: To understand the qualities that make a person a good friend.

This is a guessing game in which the class have to guess who is being described from the information that is given to them. A person is chosen to start the game. The chosen person then has to describe someone in the class by saying three things about them – something about their appearance, something the person is good at and a quality that the person has which makes them a good friend, e.g. they are cheerful, reliable, always there when you need them, honest, caring. The person in the class who guesses correctly then has a go.

After a set number of people have had a turn, discuss the qualities that people described which make people good friends.

WHAT MAKES A GOOD FRIEND? (Years 3 and 4 writing/ discussion)

Aim: To consider the qualities that a good friend has.

Ask the children to work in groups of four or five. Give each group a piece of paper, Ask them to write down five qualities that a good friend has.

Prompt them as necessary by giving examples of what they might include, e.g. A good friend...is someone you can trust to keep a secret, always shares with you, sticks up for you, likes to do what you like.

In a plenary session draw a spidergram on the board of their ideas about what qualities a good friend has.

WHAT IS A GOOD FRIEND? (Years 5 and 6 discussion)

Aim: To think about what a good friend is.

Make a series of cards with different statements on them (see below). Ask the children in turn to pick a card and to say whether or not the statement on it is true or false. Then hold a discussion in which the rest of the class say whether or not they agree.

- A good friend must always agree with me.
- A good friend must be kind and considerate.
- A good friend must have the same interests as me.
- A good friend must be willing to share.
- A good friend must be able to keep secrets.
- A good friend must be reliable.
- A good friend will let you borrow things.
- A good friend must be honest.
- A good friend should have other friends.
- A good friend will always lend you money.
- A good friend won't get cross with you.
- A good friend will stick up for you whatever you have done.
- A good friend will be willing to do whatever you ask.
- A good friend will forgive you.

WHAT SHOULD YOU DO? (Years 3–6 discussion)

Aim: To discuss what you should do when you have problems with friends.

Invite pairs to discuss these situations and compare their suggestions in a class discussion.

- Your friend wants you to go to the park, but you would rather stay in.
- Your friend has promised to play with you, but when you go round he's gone out with someone else.
- Your friend who has always sat next to you goes and sits next to someone else.
- You want to watch TV, but your friend wants to play a computer game.
- Your friend has borrowed a DVD, but won't give it back when you ask.

WHY DID YOU PULL HER HAIR? (Years 3 and 4 poem for discussion)

Aim: To discuss a situation in which a friend breaks a promise.

Why did you pull her hair?

I told my friend a secret.
She promised not to tell.
My friend told her friend.
She told her friend as well.

Now, everyone knows my secret.
I think that it's unfair.
I told my friend I trusted her.
That's why I pulled her hair.

Read the poem to the children and discuss the situation with them. Ask: Should you expect friends to be able to keep secrets? Does it depend what the secret is? Is the girl justified in pulling her friend's hair? Suggest that by pulling her friend's hair the girl in the poem only made the situation worse. What else could she have done instead? Encourage them to talk about times when they have felt very angry with a friend. How did they express their anger? Did the way they expressed their anger make the situation better or worse?

PROBLEMS WITH FRIENDS – WHAT SHOULD YOU DO?
(Years 7 and 8 discussion)

Aim: To discuss more situations involving problems with friends.

Put the list of situations (below) on the board and ask groups to discuss what you should do in each case. Then share their suggestions in a class discussion. Points to consider are: whether you should try to talk the friend about their behaviour, whether you should ignore it and hope it won't happen again, whether you should pick a quarrel with them, or ask an adult for advice.

What should you do if your friends start:

- Talking about you behind your back
- Teasing you about your appearance
- Making excuses whenever you ask them to go out or come round to your house
- Criticising the way you behave and complaining about what you do
- Going around with a different group
- Bossing you about and insisting you do what they say
- Keeping things secret from you
- Calling you a chicken because you won't join in
- Telling other people things you told them in confidence
- Being unreliable and not sticking to arrangements you made
- Getting jealous because you are being successful in some way
- Refusing to listen to your point of view?

In groups of three, role play a radio phone-in in which an agony aunt or uncle gives advice to teenagers who phone in about problems they are having with a friend. The teenager describes the problem and the presenter discusses with the agony aunt or uncle what they would advise the teenager to do.

Invite individuals to imagine they work for a teenage magazine as an agony aunt. Draft a letter that they have received about a problem someone is having with a friend and the advice that the agony aunt gives.

CLOSE FRIENDSHIPS (Years 7 and 8 discussion)

Aim: To be aware of what is acceptable in a close relationship.

Give each of the children a green card, a yellow card and a red card. Explain that you are going to read out a number of statements about people's behaviour in a close relationship. Ask them to hold up a green card if they think it is acceptable, a red card if they think it is unacceptable and a yellow card if they are unsure. After they have decided, ask them to explain the reasons for their decisions.

- It is alright to criticise your girlfriend/boyfriend.
- It is alright to feel jealous when you friend wants to spend time with their other friends.
- It is alright for your friend to want to know where you are all the time.
- It is alright to let your friend make decisions for you.
- It is alright to start going out with someone else as well, so long as you tell your friend.
- It is alright for your friend to have secrets from you.
- It is alright for you and your friend to have separate hobbies and interests.
- It is alright to lose your temper if your friend lies to you.
- It is alright to say no if your friend pressurises you to do something you do not want to do.
- It is alright if your friend posts things about you on social networking sites.

CHAPTER 4

Managing your time

This chapter consists of activities in which the children are asked to reflect on how good they are at managing their time. An initial exercise on how they spend their free time is followed by ranking exercises to discover how organised they are at home and at school. Finally, there is a game which they can play which will prompt them to think about how they may be interrupted when doing their homework and how to deal with such interruptions.

HOW DO YOU SPEND YOUR FREE TIME? (Years 3 and 4 discussion/creating a chart)

Aim: To explore how the children spend their free time.

Introduce the topic by talking with the children about how they spend their free time after school. Encourage them to talk about their interests and any hobbies or sports that they do.

Ask the children to draw a chart like the one below and set aside a time each day for them to fill in how many hours they spend on different activities after school during a week.

Ask the children to suggest the activities that they might include in the activities column such as watching TV, playing with friends, playing computer games. Others might be: visiting relatives, help-ing at home, reading, doing my hobby, playing sports, club activities, practising a musical instrument, playing with/looking after a pet.

Once the charts have been completed, groups can compare how much time individuals spend on different activities. Ask them to

How I spend my free time after school

	Hours spent				
Activity	Monday	Tuesday	Wednesday	Thursday	Friday

decide which person in the group makes the most effective use of their time.

End with a class discussion in which you point out that some activities are more productive than others and there is a need to balance the time spent on activities, such as watching TV and playing computer games with more active activities such as sports, hobbies and helping at home.

HOW ORGANISED ARE YOU AT HOME? (Years 3–6 ranking activity/ discussion)

Aim: To consider how organised they are at home.

Prepare for this game by asking each child to make cards numbered 1 to 5 with the correct number of stars on each. Explain that 1 means poor 2 means not very good 3 means average 4 means good 5 means very good. Then ask them the questions below. Each child must decide how they rate themselves and select the appropriate card and place it face down upon the table. You then choose some of them in turn to reveal their answers before going on to the next question.

How good are you at:

- Clearing away after your games
- Remembering to do your chores
- Keeping your room tidy
- Looking after your clothes
- Getting ready for school
- Taking messages and passing them on
- Remembering things to take to school
- Making arrangements and keeping appointments
- Returning things you borrow?

After playing the game, go through the list and ask the children to suggest things that they might do to help themselves become more organised at home. Points to draw out include the importance of developing routines. For example, if they find it difficult to fit in their chores, then it can be a good idea to try to do them at the same time each day. Similarly, it can be helpful to set aside a particular time each week to tidy their room or a particular time before they go to bed to put out the things they know they are going to need the following morning.

Explain that many children – and adults – spend a lot of time and energy searching for things because they can't remember where they put them down. Encourage them to tell stories about when they have lost something important and then found it in the place where they had put it down. Point out that getting into the habit of putting things away in the same place is another way of improving your organisation and is particularly useful when you are looking for items that you have borrowed and need to return, like a DVD or library book.

Talk about how to use reminders to help them to remember things. For example, do they have a note pad or notice board in their room, on which they can write notes and lists to remind them of things they have to do? Do they have a calendar on which they can write details of things they need to remember, such as arrangements they have made to go to a friend's to play or a note of when a friend's birthday is so that they won't forget to send them a card or to buy them a present.

HOW ORGANISED ARE YOU AT SCHOOL? (Years 3–6 ranking activity/discussion)

Aim: To consider how organised they are at school.

This activity is similar to the activity 'How organised are you at home?' Get the children to rank themselves in answer to the questions below using the cards numbered 1 to 5.

How good are you at:

- Being on time
- Getting out the things you need
- Getting down to work
- Clearing up
- Keeping your drawer tidy
- Looking after your belongings
- Remembering to bring things in
- Remembering to give letters to your parents?

In the follow-up discussion, two of the main points to draw out are that organisation depends largely on remembering what events and activities are going to take place and on carrying out in a methodical way tasks like getting ready, getting down to work and putting things away.

End the activity by drawing up a class set of instructions 'How to become more organised at school'.

FINDING TIME FOR HOMEWORK (Years 5 and 6 homework game)

Aim: To understand how homework may get interrupted and how interruptions can be avoided.

For this activity groups need to make a board on which to play the game and 12 interruption cards. Each group will also need counters and a dice.

First, they should make a board with 36 squares on it, consisting of a grid of six lines of six squares. The squares should be numbered 1 to 36 starting with the bottom left hand square. An 'I' should be written on the following numbers 3, 6, 8, 10, 11, 17, 19, 24, 29, 30, 33, 34.

The 12 interruption cards need to have the following instructions written on them:

- It is your turn to take the dog for a walk. Miss 2 turns.
- You are playing computer games and you lose track of time. Go back 4 spaces.
- Your friend texts you and you exchange texts with her. Miss a turn.
- A friend calls round and you go to the park with him. Miss 2 turns.
- You sit and watch TV. Miss a turn.
- You have to phone a friend because you can't remember what the homework is. Go back 3 spaces.
- A relative comes round and you are expected to talk to them. Miss a turn.
- You can't find the books you need. Go back 3 spaces.
- You fall asleep on the sofa. Go back 2 spaces.
- You have to go to your judo class. Miss a turn.
- Your dad orders you to clean your bike. Go back 3 spaces.
- Your sister has had an accident, so you have to go to the hospital. Miss a turn.

Before you begin, shuffle the interruption cards and put them in a pile.

Explain that the object of the game is to get your homework done by reaching square 36.

You take it in turns to throw the dice and to move your counter. Each time you land on a square with an 'I' on it, you have to take an interruption card and follow the instructions on it.

The purpose of the game is to show how many things can get in the way of doing homework. After playing the game, talk about the various interruptions that can occur and how they need to be aware of them. Which of the situations that interrupted them were due to circumstances beyond their control? Which interruptions were situations that they could have done something about? How could they have handled these situations so that they did not interrupt their homework?

Ask the children to role play a scene in which three children try to persuade one of their friends to go out with them instead of staying in to do his homework. Get some of the groups to show their role plays to the rest of the class. Ask whoever was playing the part of the person under pressure what it felt like and how difficult it was to say 'no'.

CHAPTER 5
Understanding your emotions

The activities in this chapter are designed to help children understand their emotions. Initial activities for younger children focus on the different feelings people have and how these feelings are expressed. There are then separate activities on feelings of anger, guilt, grief, anxiety and embarrassment.

OUR FEELINGS (Years 3 and 4 discussion)

Aim: To understand the different feelings that people have.

Introduce the topic by explaining that we all have different feelings at different times, depending on lots of things, such as whether we are well or ill, whether we are doing something we like or having to do something we don't like, and on how people treat us.

Ask what different kinds of feelings do people have and list the feelings the children suggest on the board. Prompt them as necessary by asking questions such as: How do you feel when someone gives you a present? How do you feel if a trip you have been looking forward to is cancelled? How do you feel if a pet is ill or someone in your family has to go into hospital?

Draw a circle of feelings. On one side of the circle list pleasant feelings and on the other side list unpleasant feelings. Your lists might look like this: happy, excited, pleased, safe; confident, eager, grateful; sad, disappointed, frightened, jealous, angry, guilty, anxious, bored, worried, lonely, frustrated.

Prepare a set of cards with a different feeling written on each one. Play pass the bean bag. When the music stops, ask the person holding the bean bag to draw a card and read out the feeling that is written on the card. The person then has to think of a time when they experienced that feeling. Then he passes the bean bag to the person next to him who has to think of a time when they had that feeling. Continue round the circle till everyone has had a chance to speak. Children can pass, if they can't think of anything to say. When everyone has spoken who wishes to do so, repeat the exercise by passing the bean bag again and getting someone to draw another card from the pack.

EXPRESSING FEELINGS (Years 3 and 4 making a collage/role play)

Aim: To understand how people show their feelings through their expressions and body language.

Talk about how we express our feelings by our expressions and gestures and by the way we behave. Begin by asking the children individually to express different feelings on their faces, then ask them to move around, making gestures which express different feelings.

Give out some old magazines. Ask the children to search for pictures of faces that express different feelings. Either mount them separately for display or produce a collage of faces showing different emotions.

Invite pairs or groups to role play situations involving different feelings, e.g. getting a pleasant surprise, hearing some disappointing or sad news, feeling anxious about having to do something for the first time. Ask some of them to perform their role plays and talk about similar situations they have encountered during their lives.

HOW DO THEY FEEL? (Years 3 and 4 discussion/mime)

Aim: To help the children understand other people's feelings and to empathise with them.

Read the scenarios below. For each scenario, ask how the children would feel if they were Sam. Encourage them to mime Sam's feelings by their expression and body language.

Scenario 1   It is Jim's birthday. Sam is one of his group of friends. He is looking forward to being asked to Jim's party.

Scenario 2   Sam hears the other friends in the group talking about having received invitations to the party, but Sam has not received one.

Scenario 3   The day before the party Jim comes up to Sam and gives him an invitation. Jim says he couldn't understand why Sam hadn't replied, then he found Jim's invitation still in his bag.

Repeat the activity by asking them to imagine they were Rosie in the following scenarios.

Scenario 1   Rosie's gran is rushed to hospital. Rosie and her family spend the evening at the hospital.

Scenario 2   Rosie goes to school next day to do a test, but cannot concentrate.

Scenario 3   Rosie's gran is a lot better when they go to see her again.

Scenario 4   Rosie gets a low grade in the test. She hears some of the girls sniggering because she did badly.

Scenario 5   The girls who were sniggering hear about Rosie's gran being ill. They go up to Rosie and apologise.

WHAT MAKES YOU ANGRY? (Years 3–6 discussion)

Aim: To understand what makes people angry.

Ask the children to think about what makes them angry. Ask pairs or groups to list what makes them angry, then collect their ideas on the board. Put the list of 'Things that make me angry' (below), which was drawn up by a year 4 class, on the board and compare it with their lists.

Things that make me angry

I get angry when. . .

I'm not allowed to do what I want to do.

someone bosses me about.

I don't win.

I'm accused of something I didn't do.

someone calls me a name.

I get told off and it wasn't my fault.

I'm very tired and hungry.

someone spoils my game.

I can't have something I want.

my friend won't do what I want.

I'm jealous because my sister gets more attention than me.

someone lets me down.

Ask the children each to pick out two things from the lists that make them angry. Talk about times when they have felt very angry. How did they express their anger?

DEALING WITH FEELINGS – ANGER (Years 3–6 discussion/ writing)

Aim: To understand how to deal with feelings of anger.

Discuss how feeling angry can sometimes make us lose our temper and do something we later regret. Encourage them to share experiences of when they have been very angry and said or done something they later regretted.

Point out that there are basically three ways of behaving when we are angry:

- We can take it out on other people or things – by stamping, swearing and shouting, kicking and punching, slamming doors and breaking things.
- We can try to understand our anger, listen to what other people have to say and see if we can use our anger in a positive way.
- We can sulk and bottle up our anger.

Put the list of Dos and Don'ts on how to deal with anger on the board. Ask groups to discuss the lists and to decide which are the three best pieces of advice.

DO	DON'T
Stop and think before you do or say anything.	Start shouting or swearing and calling people names.
Think about why you feel so angry.	Kick or punch anybody.
Tell somebody why you are so angry.	Slam doors, throw things or break things.
Listen to whoever made you angry – try to understand their point of view.	Refuse to listen to what other people have to say.
Get rid of your anger by punching a pillow rather than punching or kicking somebody.	Go into a sulk and bottle up your anger.

DEALING WITH FEELINGS OF GUILT (Years 3–6 a ranking activity)

Aim: To understand why people may feel guilty and how to deal with feelings of guilt.

Make a number of cards which describe situations (see the list below) in which a child might feel guilty. Ask groups to put the cards in order of how guilty each situation would make them feel.

- Borrowing something and pretending you've lost it so you can keep it
- Accidentally breaking a toy of your brother's and denying you did it
- Skateboarding on the pavement and knocking over a small child
- Spreading a false rumour about a friend who has made you angry
- Not turning up for a football match and letting the team down
- Lying to your parents about where you are going
- Taking a bar of chocolate from a shop without paying
- Letting your brother or sister take the blame for something you did
- Cheating in a test
- Sending a nasty text message to someone you don't like
- Doing nothing when a friend is being bullied.

You can also give out some blank cards and encourage the children to think of other situations in which they might have felt guilty, to write the situations on cards and to decide how guilty each situation would make them feel.

Compare their views in a class discussion. Talk about each situation in turn and discuss what they could do to make amends.

FEELING GUILTY (Years 5–8 role play/thought tracking)

Aim: To understand what it is like to feel guilty.

Ask the children to choose one of the situations and to role play a scene in which the guilty child is asked by an adult about what they did. Get them to pause the role play, when you say PAUSE and ask the guilty person to say what they are thinking and feeling at that moment.

DEALING WITH ANXIETY – A WORRIES THERMOMETER
(Years 3–6 discussion)

Aim: To understand how some worries and feelings of anxiety are less serious than others.

Explain that everyone gets anxious or worried at times and that a survey of children's worries found that their worries varied from being concerned about ill relatives and about parents rowing, to worries about tests, doing something new or being chosen for the football team.

Give groups a large piece of paper, some sheets of A4 paper, a pair of scissors, a pot of glue and a felt tip pen. Ask them to draw a large thermometer at the side of the large piece of paper and to cut the sheets of A4 paper into strips. Then, get them to think of all the things that children get worried about and to write them on separate strips of paper.

Prompt them, as necessary, to think about worries about being late for school, getting homework done and failing tests, worries about having to move house, about going to a new school, their parents being ill or separating, about falling out with friends, getting into trouble for something they have done wrong.

When they have written the worries on the strips of paper, get them to decide how serious a particular worry is and to use the glue to stick it onto the large sheet of paper – towards the bottom if they think it relatively unimportant and towards the top if they think it is important.

Compare their thermometers in a plenary session and point out that when they are worried about something thinking about where it would come on the thermometer of worries can help you to realise that it is not something big.

HANDLING STRESS (Years 5–8 discussion)

Aim: To understand ways of handling stress.

Ask the class to suggest different ways of handling stress. Write their suggestions on cards and put the cards in a box. Some of the suggestions might be:

Talk to a friend. Talk to a parent. Talk to a teacher. Try not to think about it. Do nothing and hope it will go away. Have something to eat. Do something active. Listen to music. Watch TV or play a video game. Have a good cry. Keep it to yourself. Take a drug to feel better. Throw something or smash something.

Then ask the class to consider each of the situations (below) in turn. Invite them to draw two suggestions from the box and to discuss whether they are good or bad ways of dealing with stress. Which of the actions would be most likely to relieve the stress? Which would be most likely to make it worse?

- Tricia is worried about her parents separating.
- Dominic is worried that he won't be selected for the team.
- Tamsin is worried that she'll fail the test.
- Aisha is worried about moving to a new school.
- Hanif is worried about having to have an operation.
- Pam is worried because her cat is ill,.
- Alec is worried because his grandfather has had a stroke.
- Charlie is worried that his school report will be bad.
- Xavier is worried because he has told a lie.
- Norma is worried because she has revealed something a friend told her in confidence.

DEALING WITH FEELINGS – GRIEF (Years 6–8 discussion)

Use the poem 'My little sister' to introduce a discussion of what it feels like to suffer a bereavement. Talk about how the person in the poem feels about her little sister. What does the poem suggest about the relationship between the two sisters? Do you think the older sister will feel guilty in any way about the relationship they had? Talk about how people often feel guilt as well as shock, anger and sadness when a family member dies.

My little sister

My little sister used to get on my nerves.

She'd borrow things without asking
then put them back in the wrong place.

When my friends came round,
she'd pester them
until they'd let her play with them.

If there was something I wanted to watch,
she'd refuse to change channels
unless I bribed her.

When she woke up in the middle of the night,
she'd crawl in beside me
and wake me up with her wriggling.

My little sister used to get on my nerves.
But the bedroom seems so empty without her
And I miss her terribly.

EMBARRASSMENT PYRAMIDS (Years 5–6 ranking activity/ discussion)

Aim: To identify situations in which people feel embarrassment and to discuss how to deal with embarrassment.

Introduce the topic by suggesting that some situations in which people feel embarrassed are more embarrassing than others. Explain the idea of a pyramid of embarrassment and invite groups to draw a pyramid on a large piece of paper. The pyramid should consist of ten blocks of stone at the bottom and one at the top.

Encourage them to think of embarrassing situations and to rate the situations on a scale of one to ten, with one being the most embarrassing. Then write each situation on a piece of paper and stick it on the pyramid putting the least embarrassing situations at the bottom of the pyramid and the most embarrassing at the top.

Prompt them to think of embarrassing situations involving parents, such as being kissed goodbye in the playground, involving relatives commenting on their appearance, involving younger brothers and sisters acting inappropriately, involving making a fool of themselves in class or saying the wrong thing.

Ask: How do people feel when they are embarrassed? Talk about how they often feel upset and confused. They may blush or start to stutter and stammer, not knowing what to do or say.

How embarrassed a person feels depends on the situation – who is present, what they did, whether it was intentional or accidental and how much they have appeared foolish or ridiculous.

Ask them in groups to discuss how best to deal with embarrassing situations. Encourage them to pick out some of the situations they included on their pyramids and to decide how they could deal with them.

End the topic by putting the statements (below) on the board and asking them to say whether they agree or disagree with them. Then ask them to decide on their top tip on how to deal with embarrassment.

- If you've made a fool of yourself, it's best to shrug your shoulders and join in laughing at yourself.
- Whatever you do, don't show you are angry at being embarrassed. Try to show it's no big deal by just ignoring what's happened and walking away.
- Acknowledge that you're embarrassed and tell yourself everyone gets embarrassed about something. Ask the person who has done or said something that embarrassed you not to do it again.

- If you're embarrassed because you've said something or done something that has hurt or offended someone else, apologise for what you did.

CHAPTER 6
Bullying

This chapter focuses on the different types of bullying from name-calling to cyberbullying. It looks at why people bully, who gets bullied, how it feels to be bullied and how to deal with bullying. There are statements to discuss, role plays to perform and letters to which they can draft answers.

WHAT IS BULLYING? (Years 3 and 4 a whole class activity)

Aim: To understand the different kinds of bullying.

Ask all the children to stand up and read out one of the actions (below). They have to decide whether the action is a form of bullying. Those who think it is put their hands up. Those who think it isn't sit down. Then ask some of them to explain why they decided it is or is not a form of bullying. Repeat the activity for each action.

- Making fun of the clothes people wear
- Calling someone by a nickname
- Spreading a rumour about someone
- Forcing someone to hand over money
- Ignoring someone by not speaking to them
- Imitating someone's accent
- Deliberately damaging someone's property
- Physically threatening somebody
- Sending insulting messages
- Saying things about a person's family
- Laughing at someone's mistake
- Punching or kicking someone
- Calling someone a loser.

Conclude the session by explaining that there are three types of bullying – verbal, emotional and physical and drawing up lists of the different types of bullying.

HOW DOES IT FEEL TO BE BULLIED? (Years 4–6 discussion)

Aim: To understand what it feels like to be bullied.

Use the poem 'And how was school today?' to introduce a discussion of what it feels like to be bullied. Ask: What is the child in the poem thinking and feeling? Make a list of words to describe the person's feelings. The list might include miserable, unhappy, dejected, depressed, rejected, lonely, excluded, alone, isolated, desperate.

And how was school today?

Each day they ask: And how was school today?
Behind my mask, I shrug and say OK.

Upstairs, alone, I blink away the tears
Hearing again their scornful jeers and sneers.

Hearing again them call me by those names
As they refused to let me join their games.

Feeling again them mock me with their glares
As they pushed past me rushing down the stairs.

What have I done? Why won't they let me in?
Why do they snigger? What's behind that grin?

Each day they ask: And how was school today?
Behind my mask, I shrug and say OK.

Explain that people are sometimes bullied because of the clothes they wear, because of the colour of their skin, because of the way they speak or because they have a disability.

Encourage the children in groups to imagine that they have been the victims of bullying. Each of them should decide why they were picked on and what form the bullying took. Then they should take it in turns to make a statement saying

1. Why they were bullied and the form that the bullying took.
   'I was bullied because...'
   'What the bullies did was...'

2. What their thoughts and feelings were when they were being bullied.
   'When I was being bullied I thought...'
   'When I was being bullied I felt...'

End the activity by asking them to share what the activity taught them about how it feels to be bullied. Points to make during the discussion include the following:

Being bullied can result in feelings of low self-esteem, make a person lack confidence and feel lonely. The person may think there is something wrong with them, become withdrawn and depressed, or they may also get angry and take it out on someone else.

WHY DO PEOPLE BECOME BULLIES? (Years 5–8 discussion)

Aim: To discuss the reasons why people become bullies.

Put the poem below on the board and ask the children if they think that people who are bullied become bullies.

I was bullied once

I was bullied once.
Now I'm a bully too.
They took it out on me,
So I'll take it out on you.

Make sets of cards on which are written reasons why people bully. Ask groups to rank the reasons, starting with the reason they think is the main reason. Include one or two blank cards so that the group can add any other reasons that they suggest.

- They feel threatened because the person they bully is cleverer than them.
- They feel resentful, because they are not as well off as the people they bully.
- Bullying makes them feel strong.
- They feel jealous of the people they bully.
- They are unhappy and it makes them feel better about themselves.
- They don't like anyone who they feel is different.
- They want to impress their friends.
- They become bullies because they have been bullied.

WHAT SHOULD YOU DO IF YOU ARE BEING BULLIED?
(Years 5–8 discussion)

Aim: To consider different ways of dealing with bullying.

Put these statements on the board and ask groups to discuss them, saying which of the two statements in each pair they agree with and why. The children can compare their views with the advice given at www.antibullyingalliance.org.uk

A. It's best to fight back otherwise they will think you are weak.

B. If you fight back, you'll only get into trouble for fighting.

C. It's best to ignore them. If they get no reaction, they'll eventually stop.

D. It's no good pretending to ignore them, they'll just keep on tormenting you.

E. If you are being bullied, you should always tell an adult.

F. You shouldn't tell tales. You have to find a way of dealing with it yourself.

G. If you see someone being bullied, you should intervene and try to stop it.

H. It's none of your business, if someone else is being bullied. You shouldn't get involved.

I. It's no good asking your friends to help. You have to deal with it alone.

J. The more people there are standing up to the bullies, the more they are likely to back off.

K. If someone sends you an insulting email or instant message, send them one back.

L. It's better to delete emails from bullies and to block the user than to start trading insults.

DEAR DOROTHY (Years 5–8 discussion/writing)

Aim: To consider what advice to give someone who is being bullied.

Invite groups to discuss how they would answer this letter. Draft a reply then share your replies in a class discussion.

Dear Dorothy

I am desperate. There are four children who go round together who are making my life a misery. They call me names and empty things out of my bag. They bump into me in the corridor and won't leave me alone. They threaten to beat me up if I tell anyone. What should I do? Jason

DEALING WITH CYBERBULLYING (Years 5–8 discussion/ hotseating/role play)

Aim: To define cyberbullying and to discuss what to do if you are the victim of cyberbullying.

Ask the class individually to write down what cyberbullying is. Then discuss their definitions and agree on a class definition of cyberbullying. Prompt them to include impersonation in their definition in addition to using the internet and other forms of digital technology to harass, threaten, embarrass or target someone.

Then ask the children to discuss what you should do if you are being cyberbullied and to draw up a list of Top Tips for dealing with cyberbullies. Prompt them as necessary to include advice such as:

- Stop using the site on which they are being bullied.
- Save any emails or text messages from the bully as evidence of the cyberbullying.
- Block the person who sent the hurtful emails or messages.
- Tell someone about the bullying. (There is clear advice on who you should inform about the different kinds of cyberbullying at www. internetmatters.org)

Other points to make include keep your passwords private and learn about privacy settings, such as how to change Facebook's default privacy setting.

Ask them to imagine they are a person who is being cyberbullied. Encourage the children to take it in turns be hotseated and to say what it feels like to be cyberbullied.

Invite the children to role play a scene in which two children are arguing about what one of them has put on the internet. One of them argues that what he put on the internet was a joke. The other person argues that it was inconsiderate, inappropriate and embarrassing.

CHAPTER 7

Managing your money

This chapter deals with the topic of money management. It includes activities on wants and needs, on selling and swapping, on making choices and on deciding what is the best buy. There is also a quiz to determine whether they are spenders or savers, budgeting activities and activities to make the children aware of the techniques that advertisers use to try to get people to buy their products.

WANTS AND NEEDS (Years 3–6 a sorting activity)

Aim: To understand the differences between wants and needs.

Prepare for the activity by making sets of cards with the following written on them:

Clothes to keep you warm	Clothes in the latest fashion
A home to live in	Your own bedroom
Nutritious food	Sweets and chocolate
Clean water	A washing machine
Clean air	A mobile phone
Medical care	Holidays
School equipment	A personal computer
A passport	A TV
A cooker	A dishwasher
Books	Comics and magazines

Put the children in groups and give each group a set of cards. Ask them to separate the cards into two groups – one of Wants, the other of Needs. Then ask them to choose the six cards which they think are the most important. Compare their choices in a class discussion and talk about what they have learned from the activity about the difference between wants and needs.

CHOICES, CHOICES (Years 3–6, discussion)

Aim: To understand that spending money involves making choices.

Ask the children how they make decisions about what to buy. Invite them to think what they would buy if a wealthy aunt gave them £50 and said that it was up to them to decide how to spend it. In addition, in order to ensure that they would make a wise choice, she was willing to give them a further £50 if they could persuade her that they had spent the £50 wisely. Discuss in groups how you would spend the £50 and choose someone to report your idea to the rest of the class. The class then vote as to whether to give you the extra £50.

SELLING AND SWAPPING (Years 3 and 4 discussion/writing/ role play)

Aim: To share views on selling and swapping their belongings.

Explain that when you are short of money, you can sometimes raise money by selling your old toys, games or DVDs. Invite groups to discuss the advantages and disadvantages of different ways of selling your possessions, such as putting them on ebay, selling them at a garage sale or a car boot sale, advertising them in a corner shop or local newspaper, offering them to your friends. Share their views in a class discussion.

Encourage the children to share their views on swapping. Begin by asking for a show of hands: Who thinks swapping is a good idea? Who thinks swapping is a bad idea? Then, put the statements (below) on the board and ask the children whether they agree or disagree with them.

'Swapping's good. If you are clever you can swap something cheap for something valuable.'

'Some people try to make you swap things. It's a form of bullying.'

'You should always get advice before you swap something.'

'There's no harm in swapping something you don't want for something you do want.'

'It depends how much things are worth. Swapping cheap things is OK. But you shouldn't swap valuable things.'

'Swapping's silly. It's too risky. The thing you get might be broken and they might refuse to take it back.'

Invite groups to draw up a list of rules for people to follow about swapping. Encourage them to present their rules as a series of 'Dos' and 'Don'ts' or lists of 'Never' and 'Always'.

Ask pairs to perform a role play in which there is an argument between two children over a swap they have made.

Finally, ask for another show of hands as to whether they think swapping is a good idea. Ask anyone who has changed their minds why they have changed their mind.

WHAT DO YOU DO WITH YOUR MONEY? (Years 7–8 budgeting activity)

Aim: To understand how they spend their money.

Ask individuals to think about how they spend their money each week. Encourage them individually to work out what percentage of their weekly income they spend on the following: sweets, snacks and drinks; comics, magazines and books; DVDs and apps; phone calls and texts; fares; sports and hobbies; toiletries and cosmetics; clothes; other expenses.

Ask them to draw a pie chart or block graph showing how they spend their money. Are they surprised by what the activity revealed about their spending pattern? If they wanted to save money, how could they alter their spending in order to do so?

THE BEST BUY (Years 6–8 research/discussion)

Aim: To understand that it pays to compare prices when buying large items.

Invite the children in pairs to imagine that they are going to buy a new bicycle, tablet or mobile phone. Ask them to discuss together what features they would like the item to have. Then use the internet to research what is available and decide what would be the best buy.

Encourage them to explain their decision to the rest of the class in a class discussion.

THE CAMPING HOLIDAY (Years 5–6 budgeting game)

Aim: To understand how the amount you have to spend determines what you can afford.

This is a budgeting game for groups of four. Get the children to make four spinners by cutting out circles of cardboard and making a hole in the centre of the card through which a pencil can be put. Then ask them to draw four sections on each card. One spinner is the campsite spinner, one spinner is the number of nights spinner, one spinner is the daily living costs (food and meals) spinner and one spinner is the activities spinner.

On the sections of the campsite spinner, ask them to write Luxury £25 per night, Good £18 per night, Standard £12 per night, Basic £5 per night. The luxury campsite has a shop, cafe, swimming pool and toilet block. The good campsite has a shop and toilet block. The standard campsite has a toilet block and the basic campsite is a farmer's field with a chemical toilet. On the number of nights spinner ask them to write 3 nights, 7 nights, 10 nights and 14 nights. On the daily living costs spinner ask them to write £15 per day, £25 per day, £40 per day, £60 per day. On the activities spinner write the costs: a visit to a theme park £80, zoo £40, swimming pool £20, beach free.

They also need to make four budget cards with £400, £600, £800 and £1000 on them.

They start the game by drawing one of the budget cards. In turn, they spin each of the spinners. They have to work out whether or not they can afford the holiday that the spinners offer.

They then shuffle the budget cards and have another go.

In a debriefing session, discuss how the people with £400 or £600 in their budgets cannot afford as long a holiday, as good a campsite or as expensive activities as those with bigger budgets.

ADVERTISING – THE TRICKS OF THE TRADE (Years 6–8 discussion)

Aim: To discuss how advertisers try to influence people.

Introduce the topic by explaining that we are surrounded by advertisements and that, while advertisers may claim that the purpose of advertisements is to inform us about the products available for us to buy, their over-riding aim is to get us to spend our money and to buy whatever is being advertised.

For this activity you need to have recorded a number of TV commercials to show to the children. Show the commercials at least twice and after each showing ask the children in pairs to make notes in answer to questions, such as: What is the purpose of and audience for the advert? How does the advert try to convince people to buy the product? Does it suggest that people who buy will be happier, healthier or more popular? Does the advert use any tricks or gimmicks to try to sell the product?

Share what the children have noted down about the adverts. Talk about the tricks and gimmicks that advertisers use to try to sell their product to the people at which it is aimed.

Point out how an advert may use the appearance and the age of the people and how they are dressed to suggest what sort of people are using the product. Discuss any use they make of quotes or scientific evidence to suggest the product is worth buying. Some adverts may use humour or include a particular celebrity or tell a story. Others include a catchphrase or slogan. Adverts often include music too and the setting is also important.

End the activity by asking the children to decide which of the adverts they think is the most effective.

ONLINE ADVERTISING (Years 6–8 research/discussion)

Aim: To investigate online advertising.

Explain how the internet is not only used by advertisers to market products sold online, e.g. by Amazon and iTunes, but also the edges of the computer screen are used as advertising space for online and offline products.

Encourage the children in pairs to research online advertising by logging on to a number of popular sites and seeing what advertising appears on them.

Hold a class discussion to share what they discovered about online advertising. Discuss whether advertising on websites that are popular with children should be either controlled or banned.

DESIGN AND MAKE YOUR OWN ADVERT (Years 6–8 planning and developing an advertisement)

Aim: To understand how advertisements are made.

Invite the children to design and make their own commercial or digital advert. Talk about how they need to think about the purpose and audience for their advert and about tricks or gimmicks they might use to sell their product. Encourage them to plan their adverts by making a storyboard, before filming it or developing it on the computer.

Get them to view each other's adverts and to discuss whose worked best and why.

ARE YOU A SPENDER OR A SAVER? (Years 7 and 8 quiz)

Aim: To explore their spending habits.

Make copies of this quiz and give it to the class to complete individually by circling the answer that applies to them. Then discuss what their answers say about how good they are at handling their money. If their answers are mostly bs it suggests that they think more carefully about how they use their money than if their answers are mostly as.

1. At the end of the week do you have some money left?
    a) no b) yes
2. Do you usually have to borrow money to buy people presents?
    a) yes b) no
3. If you want a new computer game, do you ask your parents to buy it rather than save up for it yourself?
    a) yes b) no
4. If you are given a gift of £50 do you spend it all at once rather than save some of it?
    a) yes b) no.
5. When you borrow money do you always pay it back?
    a) no b) yes
6. Do you always plan what you are going to buy when you go shopping and stick to your plan?
    a) no b) yes
7. Do you buy things on impulse because you see them and let yourself be tempted?
    a) yes b) no

8. Do you always compare prices when you are buying a large item?
   a) no b) yes
9. Do you have a job or do chores to supplement your pocket money?
   a) no b) yes
10. When you go on holiday do you save up money for the holiday rather than rely on your parents to give you extra money?
    a) no b) yes

PROBLEMS WITH PURCHASES (Years 7–8 research/hotseating)

Aim: To understand what rights you have as a consumer.

Explain that when you buy something and it doesn't work or breaks after only a short time, you have the right to take it back to the shop and complain. Encourage pairs to use the internet to research what your rights are as a consumer, then choose someone to be hotseated as a consumer affairs expert to tell the people in the situations (below) what their rights are.

Situation 1 I bought a new school bag from a sports shop, but the zip broke. I've lost the receipt. Can I take it back and ask for a replacement? Toni

Situation 2 I bought a new mobile but next day I dropped it and it broke. I went into the shop and they refused to give me a new one. Monika

Situation 3 I bought a new skirt, but when I got it home I didn't like the colour. They refused to change it. Can I make them change it? Freda

Situation 4 I bought a torch from a supermarket, but it doesn't work properly. Can I get a refund? Jed

Situation 5 I bought a tablet from a second hand shop but after a week it stopped working. The shopkeeper said it was bad luck, but refused to give me my money back. Winston

Note: As consumers their rights are as follows:

Toni can ask for a replacement or her money back as the bag is not fit for the purpose for which it was sold. She doesn't need to have the receipt.

It was Monika's fault the phone broke, not that the mobile was faulty. The shop doesn't have to replace it.

The shop is within its rights not to change the skirt, as Freda just changed her mind. But some shops allow you to take back goods within a certain period and may offer you a credit note.

Jed's torch is not fit for purpose. He's entitled to a new one or a refund.

The second hand shop owner can argue that the tablet wasn't new and that it was maybe Winston's fault that it broke.

CHAPTER 8
Coping with change

This unit focuses on dealing with changes that may occur in young people's lives such as moving house or moving from primary to secondary school. There are also activities exploring the emotions children may feel when parents separate and on adjusting to life in a step-family.

MOVING HOUSE (Years 3–6 discussion)

Aim: To discuss the reasons why people move house and what you may feel when you have to move.

Ask groups to make a list of all the reasons why a family might decide to move house such as a change in family circumstances (e.g. parents are separating, the need for more space because the family is getting bigger or to move to be closer to an elderly relative who needs care), a change in financial circumstances (e.g. one of the wage-earners is made redundant) or a change in employment circumstances (e.g. mum or dad gets a new job in another part of the country). Share their lists in a class discussion and ask them: Should children have any say in whether or not a family moves house or is it the decision entirely up to the adults?

Use the poem below to initiate a discussion of what children feel about moving house.

Ask the class: What do you think the person in the poem is feeling as they look round the house for the last time? What is it like to move house?

Encourage them to talk about their experiences of moving house.

Ask: How did you feel about moving? Were you sad, excited, angry, worried? How easy was it to settle into a new neighbourhood and to make new friends?

Moving on

It's time to go.
I take one last look round.
The bare floorboards creak –
An eerie sound.

For the very last time
I close the door
Of the room that now
Isn't my room any more.

I pause on the landing.
Outside the horn blares.
Lost deep in my memories
I hurry downstairs.

I close the front door
And the house that was home
Slips into the past
Where only ghosts roam.

MOVING SCHOOLS (Year 6 discussion)

Aim: To reassure children who are anxious about changing schools.

Explain that it is natural to be nervous when you do something new and that many people are nervous about moving up to secondary school. Introduce the idea of a 'Worries box' into which the children can anonymously put postcards saying what worries them about moving up to secondary school. Give everyone in the class a postcard and ask them to write on it one thing which they are looking forward to about going to secondary school and one thing that they are worried about. Pick out the postcards randomly and discuss with the class what they are looking forward to, what their worries are and what they can do to reduce their anxieties, such as talk to people they know who are in year 7 or 8, or find out more information about whatever is worrying them.

DEAR DOROTHY (Years 6–8 discussion/writing)

Aim: To explore the different emotions that children feel when parents separate.

Explain that you are going to ask groups to draft replies to the three letters to a magazine's problem page (below). Be aware that there may be children in the class whose parents are in the process of separating or divorcing and remind the class of the ground rules that you have made about allowing children not to talk about personal experiences unless they wish to do so.

When they have drafted their replies, share their advice in a class discussion.

> I'm scared and angry. My mum's new partner has two children and I'm going to have to share a bedroom with one of them. It's not fair. If my parents really cared about me they'd have stayed together for my sake. Pat

> I was shocked when my parents said they were going to separate. Now I wonder if it's my fault. My mum has always disagreed with the way my dad treats me. Also, I'm embarrassed, how can I tell my friends? Agnelka

> My parents rowed all the time. I was relieved when they told me they were going to separate. Now they are fighting about who I'm going to live with. Who will decide? Will I have to choose? Will I still be able to see both of them? I'm so frightened and confused. Sophie

Note: In the majority of divorce cases, the parents decide who the children are going to live with and the arrangements for seeing the other parent. If parents cannot agree, a court will decide and make two orders – a residency order and a contact order. The views of the children will be taken into consideration by the court.

GOOD ADVICE OR BAD ADVICE? (Years 6–8 discussion)

Aim: To discuss how to establish good relationships in step-families.

Put the statements below on the board and ask groups to discuss them in turn and to decide whether they offer good or bad advice. Then hold a class discussion of what is good and what is bad advice. Ask: What is the best piece of advice? What is the worst?

1. Settling in to a step-family takes time. It usually takes months or even a few years rather than a few weeks. So be patient.
2. If you are having trouble with a step-brother or sister, remember that they may be having trouble adjusting to the new situation too.
3. You don't have to do what your step-father says. He's not your father.
4. You must expect your relationship with the parent you don't live with to change.
5. Try to do things that will get your parents to change their minds so that they'll get back together.
6. Don't let the parent you live with stop you from seeing your absent parent.
7. If you are really desperate, don't do anything to make the situation worse, talk to an adult about what's wrong.
8. Make excuses if you don't want to be involved in activities with your step-family. Remember they can't force you to join in.
9. Try to understand that your step-mother or step-father is a person, rather than seeing them as a threat.
10. Stand up for yourself, if you feel the people you are living with are pushing you around.

Numbers 1, 2, 6, 7, 9, 10 offer good advice. Numbers 3, 5, and 8 offer bad advice. Number 4 is good advice, for inevitably it is affected by the fact that you no longer live together. However, some children maintain a good relationship with their absent parent.

PART 2
Keeping healthy

CHAPTER 9
Body care

This chapter contains a game that younger children can play which makes them aware of what are good hygiene habits. There are also suggestions for an assembly about skin care and a quiz for older children on what are good hygiene habits during adolescence.

THE HYGIENE GAME (Years 3 and 4 board game)

Aim: To increase awareness of the importance of personal hygiene.

For this activity groups need to make a board on which to play the game and 12 hygiene cards. Each group will also need counters and a dice.

First, they should make a board with 36 squares on it, consisting of a grid of six lines of six squares. The squares should be numbered 1 to 36 starting with the bottom left hand square. An H should be written on 12 squares, e.g. 3, 6, 8, 10, 11, 17, 19, 24, 29, 30, 33, 34.

The 12 hygiene cards need to have the following instructions written on them:

- You brush your teeth every day. Go forward 3 spaces.
- You don't have a bath or shower for a fortnight. Go back to the start.
- You often don't brush your teeth for 3 or 4 days. Miss two turns.
- You wear the same socks for a week. Miss 2 turns.
- You use a deodorant every day. Take an extra turn.
- You don't wash your hands after going to the toilet. Go back to the start.

- You wash your hair twice a week. Go forward 3 spaces.
- You use the same towel for 2 or 3 weeks. Miss 2 turns.
- You use the same comb as someone who has headlice. Go back 4 spaces.
- You don't change your underwear for a week. Miss 2 turns.
- You shower every day. Take an extra turn.
- You use the same handkerchief for several days. Miss a turn.

Explain that the object of the game is to prove you take care of your body by reaching square 36.

You take it in turns to throw the dice and to move your counter. Each time you land on a square with an H on it, you have to take a hygiene card and follow the instructions on it.

The purpose of the game is to show the importance of personal hygiene – of keeping your body clean and changing your clothes regularly.

THE SMELLY SOCK EXPERIMENT (Years 3 and 4 experiment)

Aim: To show the effects of deodorants.

Get one clean sock and one dirty, smelly sock. Spray them with deodorant and put them in separate air-tight boxes for one or two days. Then invite the children to take them out and compare how they smell! Ask: What does this prove? Explain that spraying a dirty sock with deodorant will only temporarily mask the smell and is not a substitute for washing.

PLEASE WASH YOUR HANDS (Years 3 and 4 class assembly)

Aim: To understand why washing your hands is important.

Invite the class to prepare an assembly about the importance of washing your hands. Encourage them to take on the roles of various people who explain why they wash their hands. Among the people they might include are a nurse, a surgeon, a waitress, a chef, a first aider, a butcher, an assistant in a cake shop, a gardener, a farmworker. They could also include a sketch about some invented characters, e.g. Sammy Soap, Charlotte Cleanwater and Christopher Cleantowel and how they outwit the bilious Bacteria and the gut wrenching Germs and the twin villains D and V.

SKINCARE SAFETY (Years 3 and 4 class assembly)

Aim: To learn about skincare and how to stay safe in the sun.

Invite the class to prepare an assembly about skin care and how to keep safe in the sun. Hold a class discussion about how the sun can damage your skin by causing sunburn and how too much exposure to the sun's rays can lead to skin cancer. Talk about protecting yourself by following the advice to Slip on clothes that cover as much of your body as possible, to Slop on sunscreen, to Slap on a hat and to Slide on sunglasses and Seek out shade. Point out that there are many myths about sun protection such as that a fake tan darkens the skin and protects you from sun cancer, that people with olive skin are not at risk of skin cancer and that you can't get sunburnt on cloudy, cool or windy days.

Then encourage the class to think of ways they might convey information about skin safety in an assembly. They could have a narrator to introduce such characters as Sunburnt Sue and Peeling Paula who tell about how they neglected advice and were sunburnt as a result. There could be a group called The Sunwise Kids who hold up banners and offer advice about sun protection. The class could produce posters, write a cautionary tale or epitaph about Beatrice Bunn who lay too long in the sun or compose a song to perform. There could be a parade of myths about sun safety, and the myths could be exposed by a group of Myth busters. They could end by inviting questions from the audience.

HYGIENE MATTERS (Years 5–8 quiz)

Aim: To learn what are good personal hygiene habits during adolescence

Introduce the topic by brainstorming with the class why personal hygiene is important to adolescents. Points to elicit include: good hygiene habits help you to feel better about yourself, to fit in and not offend people, to avoid being made fun of and to keep fit and healthy.

Put the statements below on the board and ask the children to decide which are true and which are false. Then ask them to role play a radio phone-in programme in which a health expert answers questions about personal hygiene during puberty. Information about the causes, effects and treatment of acne can be found at www.kidshealth.org

The answers to the quiz are: 1 False, 2 True, 3 False, 4 False, 5 False, 6 False, 7 False, 8 True, 9 False, 10 False.

1. Squeezing spots and pimples is the best way of dealing with them.
2. Washing your face gently with a cloth twice a day can help control pimples.
3. Getting a lot of sun is good way of curing acne.
4. Eating a lot of chocolate and greasy foods is the main reason why people get lots of spots and pimples.
5. Your hair may become oily during puberty. Oily hair attracts dirt, so you need to wash it regularly to avoid getting nits.
6. The more you brush your hair the healthier it will be.
7. Shaving off the hair under your arms will prevent BO.
8. The best way to stay clean during puberty is to have a daily shower.
9. Flossing your teeth every day will ensure you don't have bad breath.
10. Using a toothpick causes gaps in your teeth.

CHAPTER 10

Healthy eating

This chapter contains activities for younger children to help them to identify the nutrients in different foods and to distinguish between healthy and unhealthy foods. There is a healthy meal game and a test yourself quiz to establish whether they are healthy eaters and activities about how healthy fast foods are. For older children there is a discussion activity on undereating and over-eating and a quiz on anorexia.

MATCH THE FOODS TO THE PLATES (Year 3 matching activity)

Aim: To understand the nutrients contained in different foods.

For this activity you will need enough paper plates to give each group five plates. You also need sets of cards with a different food written on each one. You can use the same ones as are suggested for use in the Healthy Meal game (see below).

Ask the children to label the five plates with the different nutrients foods contain – calcium, carbohydrates, fats, proteins, vitamins and minerals. Then give them a set of cards and ask them to put each food card on the appropriate plate, according to which of the nutrients it contains. Point out that some foods contain more than one of the nutrients. Before the children begin, give each group a number of blank cards, so that they can write the name of any food that contains more than one nutrient and place that food on more than one plate.

When they have finished, check that they have put the foods on the right plates and talk about the importance of eating a balanced diet.

AN ALPHABET OF HEALTHY FOODS (Years 3 and 4 writing/ discussion)

Aim: To distinguish between healthy and unhealthy foods.

Give groups of children a large sheet of paper and ask them to write the alphabet in capital letters down the left hand side of the paper. Then ask them to write down as many foods as they can think of beginning with each letter of the alphabet e.g. apple, asparagus for a, biscuits and burgers for b, crisps and chocolate for c and so on. Set them a time limit.

When the time is up give them a red pencil and tell them to go through their list of foods and cross out all the ones that they think are unhealthy. Then give them a green pencil and ask them to highlight the healthiest food they have written for each of the letters.

Conclude the activity by comparing their lists and discussing which foods they have chosen to cross out and which they have chosen to highlight. Ask them to give the reasons why.

THE SCHOOL DINNER MENU (Years 3–6 discussion/writing)

Aim: To understand what a healthy school dinner is.

Encourage groups to draw up a menu of school dinners for a week. Suggest that they arrange the meals in columns as follows: meat/fish/nuts, potatoes/rice/pasta, vegetables, fruit/dessert, drink.

Compare their menus and discuss whether they provide a healthy balanced diet. Have they, for example, included chips more than twice? Have they included chicken nuggets and burgers more than once? Have they included enough fruit and vegetables? Have they included desserts that are not too full of carbohydrates? Have they included sugary drinks, chocolate or crisps that should be avoided?

THE HEALTHY MEAL GAME (Years 3–6 game)

Aim: To recognise what constitutes a healthy meal.

For this game you need to ask groups to prepare two sets of cards – food cards and drink cards. On the food cards ask the children to write the names of different foods – chicken nuggets, fish fingers, soup, pasta, jacket potato, ham sandwich, burger, fried egg, chips, crisps, biscuits, bread roll, chocolate bar, sweets, cereal bar, carrots, peas, cabbage, salad, sausages, cake, ice cream, jelly, candyfloss, fresh fruit. On the drinks cards ask them to write water, milk, cola, lemonade, hot chocolate, orange squash, fresh orange juice.

Invite pairs to play the game. Shuffle the cards and place them in two piles – a pile of food cards and a pile of drinks cards. Then each player has to draw four cards from the food pile and one from the drinks pile. The players then show their cards to each other and have to decide which person has picked the most healthy meal. They then shuffle the cards and have another turn. The winner is the person who picks the highest number of healthy meals. If a pair cannot agree about who has drawn the more healthy meal, they must consult the teacher, who will decide.

ARE YOU A HEALTHY EATER? (Years 3–6 a test yourself activity)

Aim: To investigate how healthy their individual eating habits are.

Ask individuals to keep a record of everything they eat during a day, then encourage them to use the scoring system below to see how healthy their eating habits were that day.

Explain that everyone starts with 10 points, then checks to see whether they ate or drank any of the foods in the list below. They then add or subtract points to find out their total for the day. For example, anyone who had a portion of chips subtracts one point, while anyone who had a glass of milk adds a point.

A jacket potato + 1

A glass of milk + 1

An apple/other fresh fruit + 1

Unsweetened cereal or muesli + 1

A tub of yoghurt + 1

Chicken or fish + 1

Wholemeal bread/biscuits + 1

Margarine or low fat spread + 1

A portion of fresh salad/
vegetables + 1

No added salt + 1

A portion of chips – 1

A can of cola/fizzy drink – 1

A portion of tinned fruit – 1

Cereal with added sugar – 1

A bar of chocolate/packet of
sweets – 1

A pork pie, sausages or a
meat pasty – 1

A piece of cake or packet of
crisps – 1

Butter – 1

No salad or vegetables – 1

Salt added to snacks or
vegetables – 1

Explain that a score of 14 or over indicates they have healthy eating habits, 8–13 is all right, but if they scored 7 or less they probably need to think more carefully about what they eat.

HOW MUCH DO YOU KNOW ABOUT FAST FOODS? (Years 5–8 quiz/discussion/role play)

Aim: To discuss how healthy fast foods are.

Put the statements (below) on the board and ask individuals whether they think they are true or false. The answers are: 1 True, 2 True, 3 False, 4 True, 5 True, 6 True if it contains no dressing which is high in fat/ false if it contains dressing. Facts about fast foods can be found at the Child and Youth Health website www.cyh.com

1. A fast food meal can contain 1500 calories, which is over half the number of calories required daily by a healthy adult.
2. Fast foods often contain large amounts of salt.
3. Fast foods contain plenty of fibre which helps your digestive system.
4. Fast foods contain a lot of fat which can make you overweight.

5. Fizzy drinks contain lots of sugar which can cause health problems as well as tooth decay.
6. A fast food salad is as good for you as a fresh salad.

Then ask groups to discuss the view that too much fuss is made about eating fast foods and that eating fast food isn't going to do you any harm.

Role play a TV studio discussion in which a panel consisting of a nutritionist, a spokesperson from a fast food chain, a teenager and a parent discuss their views on fast foods.

THE TOP TIPS CHALLENGE (Years 5–7 discussion/writing)

Aim: To offer advice on healthy eating.

This is an activity in which groups compete against each other to produce ten healthy eating tips. Encourage them to think of different ways of presenting the tips. They could be presented as a poster, through cartoon characters in a video commercial or acted as a scene in which a family are sitting discussing the foods they like.

If necessary, prompt the children to think about the fat, sugar and salt content of foods and drinks, the importance of a balanced diet, of choosing suitable snacks, of eating regular meals and of not going on a diet without medical advice.

THE HEALTHY CAFE (Years 5 and 6 discussion/writing/role play)

Aim: To understand what are healthy foods.

Invite the children to imagine they run the Healthy Cafe, which has only healthy meals on its menus. Ask them to produce a breakfast menu and a lunch menu for the cafe.

In pairs, they can then role play an interview with the manager of the cafe. In addition to asking the manager about the foods and drinks on offer at the Healthy Cafe, the interviewer should ask the manager about which foods and drinks are not on sale and why.

DEAR DOROTHY (Years 5–8 discussion/writing)

Aim: To increase awareness of problems that can arise from overeating and undereating.

Invite the children to imagine they work on the problem page of a magazine for teenagers Ask them to discuss the following letters in groups, then individually to draft replies to them.

Dear Dorothy

My friend eats hardly anything and is very thin. She says she likes it that way. I think she may be anorexic. What should I do? Jodie

Dear Dorothy

I'm worried that I'm getting fat. People tell me that it's because I'm going through puberty. Is that true? Should I go on a diet? Max

Dear Dorothy

My friend goes on these binges when she eats lots and lots then gets rid of it all by being sick. How can I help her? I'm worried she's harming herself. Nadine

HOW MUCH DO YOU KNOW ABOUT ANOREXIA? (Years 6–8 quiz)

Aim: To increase knowledge of facts and myths about eating disorders.

Put the statements below on the board and ask the children in pairs to decide which are true and which are false. Then share the correct answers in a class discussion. Further information about anorexia can be found at the NHS Choices website and at www.b-eat.co.uk

1. You can tell by just looking at a person whether they have an eating disorder.
2. Men do not get eating disorders.
3. Eating disorders are a cry for attention.
4. Being thin will automatically make a person happy.
5. Mannequins are ridiculously thin compared to the average sized woman.
6. No one ever fully recovers from an eating disorder.
7. Most eating disorders begin because a person goes on a weight loss diet.
8. A good way to control your food intake and weight is to make yourself sick or to take laxatives.
9. Photos of models and celebrities show girls what their bodies should look like.
10. Anorexia is only about food.

Answers
1. False: Anorexics aren't necessarily thin. They can have different body shapes.
2. False: Around 10% of anorexics are men.
3. False: Weight loss may get a positive response at first, which then turns into unwanted and negative attention.
4. False: Being anorexic often results in low self-esteem and depression.
5. True: Mannequins are size 6.
6. False: About one-third never recover, about one–third manage to live with the condition and about one-third fully recover.
7. True: A diet is often what starts anorexia.
8. False: Neither vomiting nor using laxatives is good for your body.
9. False: Every person has their own body shape and it is wrong to think that your body must look like a supermodel's.
10. False: Anorexia is a mental illness and has complex psychological origins.

CHAPTER 11

Exercise and fitness

This chapter contains suggestions for younger children for putting on an assembly about why exercise is beneficial and on preparing a presentation for a healthy heart campaign. Older children are encouraged to make and to play a Top Trumps game about the value of different forms of exercise and there is a discussion activity focusing on attitudes to school sports.

WHY EXERCISE IS GOOD FOR YOU (Years 3 and 4 class assembly)

Aim: To understand how exercise keeps your body healthy.

Invite the children to prepare a class assembly. Encourage them to use reference books and the internet to find out how exercise benefits the whole body. Then ask them for their ideas about how to use the information in an assembly.

Suggest writing a song or poem that they might include about The Exercise Kids. It could begin:

> Listen to us! We're the Exercise Kids.
> Here is what we do.
> Follow our example
> And you'll stay healthy too!

Suggest including characters in the assembly who represent parts of the body such as Heather Heart, Peter Pulserate, Billy Strongbones, Lucy Lungs and Morton Muscles who explain how exercise benefits them. They could hold up posters or placards. Other characters could be the S triplets – Susie Stamina, Sally

Suppleness and Sophie Strength –and their brother Sleepwell Sid who explain how exercising gives you more energy, builds up your suppleness and strength and helps you to sleep better. There could be interviews with Colin Couch-Potato who puts on weight because he doesn't exercise enough and the breathless twins Puff and Pant, who are always out of breath when they run because they are too lazy to do any exercise.

FITNESS FACTOR TOP TRUMPS (Years 5 and 6 card game)

Aim: To understand that the beneficial effect of activities varies.

This is a game for two players.

Explain that physical fitness consists of three important ingredients – stamina, suppleness and strength – the S-factors.

The most important is stamina – staying power. Next comes suppleness or flexibility, finally comes strength, the muscle-power for lifting and shifting.

Put the chart below on the board and ask the children to make 24 separate cards – one for each activity and to write the three S-factor scores on the card, so that, for example, the badminton card looks like this:

BADMINTON

Stamina **

Suppleness ***

Strength **

Note: *means no real effect **means beneficial effect *** means very good effect **** means excellent effect

Explain that they play the game as they play Top Trumps. One of them shuffles the cards and then deals them, so that each of them has twelve cards. They then each take a card from the top of their packs. The youngest player starts by choosing one of the three categories, which he thinks is most likely to have a higher score than his opponent's card. For example if he has the badminton card he will most likely say suppleness. His opponent then reveals what the suppleness score is on his card. If it is only 1 or 2 he has to hand over the card. If it is 4, then he takes the badminton card and puts it on the bottom of his pack. If it is 3, it is a draw. The players put the two cards down on the table. They remain there until one of the players wins a round and he then picks them up as well. The game continues until one player runs out of cards and the player with all the cards is the winner.

S-factor scores

	Stamina	Suppleness	Strength
Badminton	**	***	**
Canoeing	***	**	***
Climbing stairs	***	*	**
Cricket	*	**	*
Cycling (hard)	****	**	***
Dancing (ballroom)	*	***	*
Dancing (disco)	***	****	*
Digging (garden)	***	**	****
Football	***	***	***
Golf	*	**	*
Gymnastics	**	****	***
Hill walking	***	*	**
Housework (moderate)	*	**	*
Jogging	****	**	**
Judo	**	****	**
Rowing	****	**	****
Sailing	*	**	**
Squash	***	**	**
Swimming (hard)	****	****	****
Table tennis	*	**	*
Tennis	**	***	**
Walking (briskly)	**	*	*
Weightlifting	*	*	****
Yoga	*	****	*

THE HEALTHY HEART CAMPAIGN (Years 5–8 planning a campaign)

Aim: To understand how exercise keeps the heart and body healthy.

Invite groups to imagine that they have been employed to organise the Healthy Heart campaign which is to be run during Healthy Heart week. Their job is to promote awareness of the benefits of exercise by organising events such as a super sports day and running an advertising campaign that will encourage people to exercise daily.

The advertising campaign might consist of posters for billboards, magazine and newspaper adverts and a television commercial. The super sports day might include sponsored activities such as a fun run or a sponsored swim, and competitions such as a penalty challenge or to see who can hit the longest six.

Encourage the groups to work out detailed plans, including roughs of their proposed newspaper adverts and a storyboard for their commercial together with a programme of the events for the super sports day. Invite them to take it in turns to present their plans to the rest of the class.

EXERCISE: WHAT DO YOU THINK? (Years 7 and 8 discussion/debate)

Aim: To discuss attitudes towards exercise and sports.

Encourage groups to share their views on PE lessons, school sports and taking exercise. Use the statements below to initiate discussions, before inviting the class to debate the motion 'This house believes that schools place too much emphasis on sports and sporting activities'.

- Exercise shouldn't be compulsory in schools.
- Too much fuss is made about exercising.
- We shouldn't be made to do team sports.

- We should be able to choose for ourselves what to do in PE lessons.
- There is too much emphasis on competition and competitive sports.
- We should have a chance to exercise every day.

HOW EXERCISE BENEFITS TEENAGERS (Years 7 and 8 research/writing)

Aim: To increase awareness of the physical and mental benefits of exercise.

Put the letter below on the board and invite the children in groups to draft replies to it.

Dear Dorothy

I'm putting on weight and it's depressing me. My friend says that I should take more exercise but I'm afraid of looking silly and being teased because I'm not very co-ordinated. Please help me. I don't know what to do. Helen

Ask the children to imagine that they work for a teenage magazine and they have been asked to write an article explaining what the benefits of taking exercise are. Encourage them to research the benefits of exercise on the internet and prompt them to include the mental as well as the physical benefits.

CHAPTER 12
Smoking

This chapter focuses on attitudes to smoking, on why people smoke and the costs and effects of smoking. Children are encouraged to design a questionnaire and to carry out an investigation into people's views on smoking and there are activities on the laws about smoking and on electronic cigarettes.

WHAT DO YOU THINK ABOUT SMOKING? (Years 3 and 4 circle activity)

Aim: To discuss attitudes to smoking.

Go round the circle and ask the children in turn what they think about smoking. Explain that you are going to read out a series of statements about smoking. If they agree with the statement they should stand up. If they disagree, they should remain seated. After they have decided, invite some of them to say why they agree or disagree.

- Smoking damages your health.
- Smoking is a waste of money.
- It doesn't bother me if my parents smoke.
- Adults shouldn't smoke in front of children.
- People shouldn't smoke indoors.
- People who want to smoke should be able to do so wherever they like.
- People who become ill from smoking should have to pay for their medical treatment.
- Children who want to smoke should be able to buy cigarettes.
- People who sell cigarettes to children should be stopped from selling cigarettes.
- There's too much fuss about smoking.

WHY DO PEOPLE START TO SMOKE? (Years 3–6 discussion)

Aim: To explore the reasons why people start to smoke.

Invite pairs to write down the reasons they think people start to smoke, then hold a class discussion of their views. Points that might be made in the discussion include: pressure from friends, to appear grown up, to look cool, to do something rebellious, to try something new, excitement, their parents are smokers.

SMOKING – THE RISKS AND THE COST (Years 5–7 discussion)

Aim: To understand the risks and the costs of smoking.

Up-to-date facts and statistics about the risks and costs of smoking can be found at the Action on Smoking and Health website www.ash.org Explain that over 100,000 people a year in the UK die from smoking-related illnesses and that a person who smokes is likely to die six to nine years earlier than a non-smoker.

Ask the children to divide a piece of paper into two columns, labelled Risks and Costs and in pairs to list what they consider to be the risks and costs of smoking. Then hold a class discussion and list the points they make on the board.

Points about the risks should include: Smoking can cause cancer, lung diseases and coronary heart disease, leading to premature death. Smoking can cause addiction to nicotine. Smoking can affect your appearance – your skin, hair, teeth, hands. There is a risk to non-smokers from passive smoking.

Points about the cost should include: Smoking is expensive. Smoking costs the NHS large sums in treatment of smoking-related illnesses. Millions of working days are lost each year because of smoking-related illnesses. Fifty per cent of fatalities from domestic fires are caused by matches or other smoking materials. Smoking causes pollution.

SAYING 'NO' TO SMOKING (Years 6–8 discussion/role play)

Aim: To discuss ways of saying 'no' when offered a cigarette.

Hold a class discussion about how it can be difficult to refuse to join in when a group of friends are putting pressure on you to smoke. Discuss ways of saying 'no' assertively. For example, give them a reason. E.g. 'No thanks, I've seen the effects it can have.' 'I'd rather not take the risk, thanks.' Ask them to role play a scene in which a person is put under pressure to have a cigarette by a group of friends, then to take it in turns to act out their scenes to the rest of the class.

Discuss with the class the arguments they would use to try to persuade a friend, who has started to smoke, to give up. List their suggestions on the board, then invite pairs to role play a scene in which a person tries to persuade a friend to stop smoking.

SMOKING AND THE LAW (Years 7 and 8 research/discussion)

Aim: To understand the laws about smoking.

Ask pairs to research the laws about smoking in the UK: Where is smoking banned? What are the laws on the sale of tobacco and the advertising of tobacco? What must cigarette packets carry? What controls are there on e-cigarettes? How do laws in the UK compare with the laws in other countries? Ask pairs to share their views on whether the laws should be changed in any way in groups. Then invite groups to report their views in a class discussion.

SMOKING HABITS AND ATTITUDES (Years 7 and 8 research/writing)

Aim: To investigate smoking habits and attitudes towards smoking.

Invite the children to design a questionnaire or to use the questionnaire below to interview people to find out about their smoking habits and attitudes towards smoking. Encourage them to analyse their findings by looking at whether there is a difference between the answers given by smokers and non-smokers, by young people and older people, by males and females. Hold a class discussion in which they share what they found out. They can then each use the information they collected to write an article for a teenage magazine – 'What they say about smoking'.

Smoking questionnaire

Date of interview: Male / Female

Age: Under 11 / 11–16 / 16–21 / Over 21

		Yes	No
1.	Do you smoke? If no, go straight to question 7.	_____	_____
2.	How many cigarettes do you smoke each day?	_____	
3.	At what age did you start to smoke?	_____	
4.	Would you like to give up smoking?	_____	_____
5.	Have you ever tried to give up smoking but failed?	_____	_____
6.	Are you worried that you might become ill from smoking?	_____	_____
7.	Are you worried about passive smoking?	_____	_____
8.	Do you think health warnings on cigarette packets are effective?	_____	_____
9.	Should smoking be banned in all public places?	_____	_____
10.	Should all forms of tobacco advertising be banned?	_____	_____
11.	Do you think e-cigarettes are a good alternative to ordinary cigarettes?	_____	_____
12.	Should e-cigarettes be banned until more is known about their long-term effects?	_____	_____

E-CIGARETTES (Years 5–8 research/discussion)

Aim: To investigate issues concerning e-cigarettes.

Introduce the topic of e-cigarettes by asking the children what they know about e-cigarettes. Encourage them to find out all they can about e-cigarettes. Then hold a class discussion of these questions: Do you think e-cigarettes encourage young people to take up smoking? Do you think e-cigarettes offer smokers a way of giving up tobacco and reducing the risks of smoking? Should e-cigarettes only be available from chemists? Should e-cigarettes be banned until more is known about whether they damage your health?

CHAPTER 13
Drinking

This chapter contains a matching game about the effects of alcohol on the human body and a true or false quiz for younger children. For older children there are activities on the risks of getting drunk and on attitudes towards alcohol.

WHAT EFFECT DOES ALCOHOL HAVE ON YOUR BODY?
(Years 3–6 matching game)

Aim: To understand the effects of alcohol on the human body.

This is a memory game which teaches about the effects of alcohol on the human body. The website www.talkaboutalcohol.com has a factsheet on alcohol and further teaching ideas. The NHS Choices website www.nhs.uk has an interactive quiz – Alcohol myth buster – which you can encourage the children to do individually.

Get the children to make two sets of cards. On one set, ask them to write the names of the following parts of the body – brain, heart, liver, stomach, eyes, mouth, skin, legs.

On the other set of cards, ask then to write down what effect alcohol has on the different parts of the body:

- Slows down the speed at which the brain works.
- Heavy drinking can weaken the heart.
- Slurs speech. Heavy drinking can cause mouth and throat cancer.
- Damages liver. Heavy drinkers may need liver transplant.
- Increases blood flow to the skin, causing heat loss.
- Irritates stomach causing ulcers.

- Affects co-ordination, causing difficulty walking straight.
- Affects eyesight so that you do not see clearly.

Ask the children to join up with a partner and shuffle their two sets of cards together, then lay them face down on the table. The children take it in turns to turn over the cards. If they turn up two matching cards, e.g. liver and Damages liver. Heavy drinkers may need a liver transplant, they keep the two cards and have another turn. The winner is the person who has the most cards at the end of the game.

HOW MUCH DO YOU KNOW ABOUT ALCOHOL? (Years 3–6 quiz)

Aim: To increase knowledge of alcohol and its effects.

Challenge groups to test how much they know about alcohol. The website www.drinkaware.co.uk has details of alcohol-related road accidents.

Put these statements on the board and ask them individually to say whether they are true or false.

1. Alcohol is a drug.
2. Wine and beer contain the same amount of alcohol.
3. Alcohol is a food.
4. People over the age of 14 can go into pubs and buy alcohol.
5. Drinking alcohol when pregnant can affect the baby's development.
6. It is illegal to drive a car after drinking any alcohol.
7. Alcohol cannot be advertised on TV.
8. You can be arrested for being drunk and disorderly.
9. Alcohol is a major cause of road traffic accidents.
10. A person who gets a hangover from drinking too much alcohol is an alcoholic.

Explain that they get one point for a correct answer, but they lose two points for a wrong answer. The group with the most points is the winner.

The answers are: 1 True, 2 False, 3 True, 4 False, 5 True, 6 False, 7 False, 8 True, 9 True, 10 False.

GETTING DRUNK – THE RISKS (Years 7–8 discussion/ designing a comic strip)

Aim: To understand the risks of getting drunk.

Ask groups to draw a spidergram showing the risks involved in drinking too much.

Then pool their ideas in a class discussion and draw a class spidergram on the board.

Do or say things you'll regret	Get into a fight	Get into trouble with the police
Vomit or lose consciousness	Slur your speech	Walk unsteadily
Make a fool of yourself	**GETTING DRUNK**	Be unable to concentrate
Fall and injure yourself	Cause an accident	Get robbed
Cause damage to property	Be admitted to hospital	Lose self-control

Children in pairs can then design and produce a comic strip telling the story of a teenager and what the consequences are of the teenager getting drunk.

ALCOHOL – WHAT DO YOU THINK? (Years 5–8 TV discussion)

Aim: To explore attitudes towards alcohol and drinking.

Ask the children to imagine they are a panel of guests on a TV programme called 'Cause for concern' which is focusing on alcohol. The presenter of the programme asks the panel whether they agree or disagree with the following statements:

'I don't see what's wrong with drinking a lot and getting drunk.'

'People exaggerate the dangers of alcohol.'

'Alcohol is OK – provided you don't drink too much.'

'The world would be a better place if no one drank any alcohol.'

'Alcohol causes a lot of unhappiness.'

'Anyone who drinks too much is taking a risk.'

'People who drink alcohol lead more exciting lives than people who don't.'

As a follow-up activity you can ask individuals to pick out one statement they strongly agree with and one statement they strongly disagree with and to explain their reasons in a group discussion.

CHAPTER 14
Drugs and drug-taking

This chapter consists of activities that highlight the differences between medicines and illegal drugs. There are activities which explore why people take illegal drugs, what an addiction is, what effects drugs have on drug-takers and their lives and the laws about drugs. There are also opportunities to discuss myths and facts about drugs and what to do in various situations involving drug-taking.

THE BAG (Years 3 and 4 – discussion/role play)

Aim: To make children aware that drugs may be either medicines or illegal drugs.

This is a starter activity that can be used to introduce the topic of drugs. It can be used to start a discussion about drugs as medicines, since some children will probably suggest that the bag is full of prescribed drugs, as well as a discussion about illegal drugs.

Ask the children to imagine they are playing hide-and-seek in the park when one of them finds a plastic bag full of tablets. Discuss what the tablets might be and who they think they might belong to. Encourage the children to discuss the questions below.

- What do they think the person who the bag belongs to might be going to do with the tablets?
- Who might buy the tablets if the person tried to sell them?
- How would they know that the tablets were what the person said they were?
- What effect might the tablets have on a person who took them?
- What do you think the children should do with the bag of tablets?

Ask them in groups to role play a scene in which the children argue about what to do with the bag.

TAKING CARE WITH MEDICINES (Years 3 and 4 discussion/ role plays)

Aim: To understand the need to take care with medicines.

Encourage the children to talk about medicines that they have been prescribed during their lives and point out that drugs are used to cure infections, to control diseases such as asthma and diabetes and to reduce pain, for example if you have a painful injury, such as a broken bone. Talk about how drugs can also be used as vaccines to prevent you from getting an infectious disease.

Explain that we must take care with medicines, for example, by only taking the amount the doctor tells us and by not leaving them where babies and toddlers may find them.

Invite them in pairs to role play the following situations and to decide what is the safest thing to do.

- You are staying at a friend's. You get a sore throat. The friend's mother offers to give you some medicine.
- Your doctor gave you some ointment when you cut yourself badly. You have grazed your knee. Your parents are out. Your brother suggests you put some of the ointment on your knee.
- You have taken some medicine which the doctor has given you, but you have come out in a rash and it makes you feel sleepy. You tell the babysitter.
- Your two-year old sister has found a bottle of pills and scattered them on the floor. You can't be sure whether she has swallowed any. You discuss with your older sister what you should do.

Discuss where medicines should be stored and invite them to draw posters to encourage people to store medicines safely.

WHAT EFFECTS DO DRUGS HAVE? (Years 5–8 research/role play)

Aim: To explore what effects illegal drugs can have.

Invite groups to investigate the effects that illegal drugs can have on a person's life. Encourage different groups to research different effects. For example, group A's task can be to find out and explain the physical effects that drugs can have on a person's body. Group B's task can be to investigate the effects that drug-taking can have on a family's life. Group C can concentrate on the effects that drug-taking can have on schoolwork or a person's job. Group D can look into how drug-taking can lead to involvement in crime.

Each group can then take it in turn to explain what they have found out to the rest of the class. They can do this in role. For example, group A can be a group of doctors, group B can be family members, group C can be teachers and group D can consist of police officers, magistrates and social workers.

HABITS AND CHOICES (Years 5 and 6 discussion)

Aim: To understand what an addiction is and the idea of choice in addiction.

Explain that some of our behaviour takes place without our thinking about it and some by choice. Give pairs this list of actions and ask them to decide which are involuntary actions – actions we do without thinking – and which are voluntary actions – actions we do by choice.

Then discuss which of the actions can become a habit that we may find difficult to control and which can become addictions.

Breathing, putting on makeup, chewing pencils, nailbiting, fiddling with your hair, eating, thinking, taking exercise, tapping your foot, smoking, taking pills, yawning, drinking alcohol, getting dressed, coughing, tipping your chair back, taking drugs.

DRUGS AND THE LAW (Years 6–8 research/role play)

Aim: To understand what the laws are about drugs.

Explain that the law divides drugs into three categories according to how dangerous they are considered to be. Class A is the most dangerous, Class B and Class C – and it is against the law to possess or supply them. There are also other drugs, which it is not illegal to sell or possess e.g. solvents.

Encourage them to research which drugs are in which category and to make a chart showing what class each drug is in.

Invite children in groups of three to role play being magistrates and to decide what sentences they would give in the cases below. Point out that there are a range of non-custodial sentences as well as custodial sentences they could give, such as a fine, community service or supervision order.

- A 20 year old convicted of selling cocaine.
- A 16 year old who has been found to have in his possession a considerable amount of cannabis.
- A 14 year old who has been selling ecstasy tablets.
- An 18 year old who is in possession of a small amount of heroin.

WHY DO SOME PEOPLE TAKE DRUGS? (Years 5 and 6 discussion)

Aim: To explore the reasons why people start to take illegal drugs.

Prepare sets of cards for each group on which are written various reasons that are suggested to explain why some young people take drugs. Groups discuss each reason and make three piles of cards according to whether they think it is one of the main reasons, quite often the reason or not often the reason. Then, get them to compare their views in a class discussion.

Reasons why some people start to take drugs:

- They see others doing so and copy them.
- They want to rebel.
- Someone dares them to do it.
- Boredom.
- To show off.
- It's against the law and it gives them a thrill.
- Curiosity.
- They think it makes them appear grown up.
- They want to take risks.
- They don't want to be left out of the group.
- They are unhappy and it will help them forget their problems.
- They can't stop. They tried it once and became addicted.
- Friends pressurise them to join in.
- They like the feelings it gives them.
- They think people exaggerate the risks.

DRUGS – FACTS AND MYTHS (Years 5–8 making graffiti walls)

Aim: To understand facts and myths about drugs and drug-taking

Split the class into groups so that there are three groups of Factfinders and three groups of Mythmakers. Give each group a large sheet of poster paper. Explain that the groups of Factfinders have the task of writing graffiti which warn people against drug use by stating facts about the illegal use of drugs. The groups of mythmakers have the task of writing graffiti which are misleading because they are myths about drugs and drug-taking. Encourage them to use the internet to check facts as necessary.

The groups then show their posters to each other and discuss the graffiti they have written, before displaying the posters on the classroom wall.

WHAT SHOULD YOU DO? (Years 7 and 8 discussion)

Aim: To discuss how to deal with situations involving drugs.

Invite groups to discuss the scenarios (below) and to decide what they would do in each case.

- You overhear your elder sister telling her friends that she is going clubbing and plans to buy an ecstasy tablet.
- A friend says she has some cannabis and encourages you to try some.
- You are in your brother's bedroom looking for something of yours which he borrowed and you find a packet of white powder in a drawer.
- A friend has started to behave oddly and you think she may be using drugs.
- An older boy has started to hang around the road opposite the school and you think he is supplying drugs.

CHAPTER 15

Growing and changing

This chapter focuses on the changes that take place in girls' and boys' bodies during puberty, on the concerns young people often feel about these changes and on how the media influence how young people view these changes.

HOW YOUR BODY CHANGES (Years 3–6 drawing a timeline)

Aim: To understand how the body changes from babyhood and in adolescence.

Introduce the activity by talking about all the changes that take place as you grow from a baby into adulthood. Invite individuals to draw a timeline showing how their body has changed so far and how it will change in the future as they go through puberty. Encourage them to include changes such as when they grew milk teeth, how they started to walk and talk, how they have grown taller, how their milk teeth have come out and been replaced and the changes they will experience during adolescence as they go through puberty. Tell them if they are unsure about any changes that will occur to use the internet to research them by reading 'All about puberty' at www.kidshealth.org.

AM I NORMAL? (Years 6–8 questions box)

Aim: To answer children's worries and concerns about the changes that occur during puberty.

Give each member of the class an index card or small piece of paper. Remind them of the changes that take place in their bodies during puberty. Explain that many children worry about whether the changes they experience are normal. Encourage them to write down any questions they have about their bodies and the developments that take place during puberty. Tell them if they can't think of any questions to write 'I have no questions' on the card or piece of paper. Pass round a container e.g. a shoebox with a slot cut in the lid. They can then post their cards or pieces of paper into the box. Getting those without any questions to put their cards/pieces of paper in the box, prevents those with questions they want answering from feeling embarrassed about asking and protects their anonymity.

In addition to the questions asked by the children, you can put questions into the box that previous groups have asked, such as:

- I'm 14 but haven't got my period yet. Is this normal?
- Can tampons get stuck?
- I get moody around the time of my period. Is it PMS?
- Is it OK to have one breast larger than the other?
- I sometimes wake up with an erection. Is this normal?
- I've had the other changes you get in puberty, but I'm still the smallest boy in our class. Am I normal?
- What activities must I avoid when I've got my period?
- My dad says boys put on weight and they sometimes look as if they're developing breasts. Is this true?
- I sweat profusely and keep on having to wash and use deodorant. Is this normal?

Hold a discussion session in which you pick out the questions and answer them. Look at the questions beforehand and use the internet to check on any answers that you do not know. The answers to most questions about what is normal at puberty can be found at the Sexual Health Advice Centre, based at Addenbrooke's Hospital, Cambridge, which has information on both boys' and girls' bodies at www.cuh.org/Addenbrookes

BODY IMAGES (Years 7 and 8 making collages)

Aim: To understand how the media present ideals of femininity and masculinity.

Explain that teenage magazines and the media in general present an idealised picture of what it means to be feminine and what it means to be masculine.

Collect copies of old magazines and distribute them to groups. Ask them to make two collages – one of the ideal feminine woman and one of the ideal masculine man. While they are looking for pictures to cut out and include ask them to think about the following questions: What makes her/him ideal? Is it because of how she/he looks? Is it because he/she looks wealthy? Fit? Well-dressed? Young? Friendly? Is it because of what she/he is doing? What makes her 'feminine' and him 'masculine'? Encourage them to comment on the pictures by including words and phrases in their collages.

Then invite them to take it in turns to present their collages to the rest of the class and to discuss what effect they think these media images have on how young people view their changing bodies.

CHAPTER 16
Keeping safe

This chapter focuses on safety issues. There are activities to make children aware of safety in the home and where to play safely out of doors, and suggestions for an assembly about how to stay safe in the street.

Other activities suggest how to act in emergencies, and deal with firework safety, water safety and how to stay safe online.

PLAY SAFE (Years 3 and 4 hotseating activity)

Ask the children to imagine that a group of them are out playing, when one of them suggests doing one of the following things: standing on a railway bridge and trying to drop stones on a passing train, looking for things that may have been thrown onto a fly-tip, exploring a derelict house, going for a swim in a lake, climbing a fence into a deserted building site, having a skateboard race in a car park. One of the group is against the idea. Encourage them to take it in turns to be hotseated as the person who is against the idea.

SARAH SENSIBLE SAYS (Years 3 and 4 class assembly)

Invite the children to prepare a class assembly giving tips on keeping safe when you are out and about. Hold a class discussion of things you should always do when you are out and about, such as always tell an adult where you are going and what time you will be back. Points to raise in the discussion include: don't take shortcuts down deserted alleyways and lanes when you are alone, keep to busy streets, don't wear headphones and be aware of traffic.

Talk about how they might present these tips in the assembly through a character called Sarah Sensible and by making placards.

Encourage different groups to discuss what you should do in various situations:

- What should you do if you are out playing and you get separated from your friends?
- What should you do if you are going to walk down a dark road at night?
- What should you do if you get lost?
- What should you do if you think someone is following you?
- What should you do if you think a car is following you?

Ask each group to think about how they can present their tips in the assembly e.g. as a role play of a family discussion, or one child telling his group of friends about what he did in that situation.

You can also work with the children to draft 'The Safety First Rap', which they can perform as part of the assembly. You can use the following four lines as the start of the rap:

Listen to me children, and do as I say
And you'll keep yourself safe when you go out to play
Put your hands together and give us a clap
And be sure to join in the safety first rap.

SAFETY IN THE HOME (Years 3 and 4 discussion/drawing/ making a collage)

Ask the children in groups to discuss which is the most dangerous place in the house. Encourage them to draw a chart with columns labelled kitchen, living room, stairs, bathroom and bedroom and get them to list all the dangers that there are in that room.

Prompt them to think of the dangers of getting burns or scalds, of falling or getting a cut and the dangers of electrical appliances.

Explain that the most common type of accidents in the home are falls. Encourage the children to talk about accidents they have had at home and how they might have been avoided.

Individuals could draw picture strips or posters warning people about the dangers at home.

They could cut pictures from old catalogues and make a collage of items, such as knives, scissors and screwdrivers, and appliances, such as electric fires, irons and other appliances that are potential dangers in the home.

SAFETY FIRST RULES (Years 3 and 4 discussion)

Aim: To understand the reasons behind safety rules.

Make copies of the list of safety rules below to give to each of the children, leaving a space beneath each of the rules. Ask them individually or in pairs to write the reason for the rule in the space provided.

Rule: When you fill a bath or sink, always put the cold water in first.

Rule: Never leave toys or books lying on the stairs.

Rule: Never play with plastic bags.

Rule: Always carry scissors with the blades shut in your hands.

Rule: Do not touch anything electrical if your hands are wet.

Rule: Never take a plug out without switching off the power first.

Rule: Never run when carrying something hot or sharp.

Rule: Do not take anything electrical into the bathroom.

WATER SAFETY (Years 3 and 4 quiz)

Aim: To be aware of the dangers when playing in or near water.

Give the children the quiz below to complete individually or in pairs. Then share their answers in a class discussion.

1. Why should you never go swimming alone?
2. Why should you not dive into unknown waters?
3. Why can it be dangerous to swim in a river?
4. Why is it dangerous to swim in very cold water?
5. Why can jumping in and out of strong waves be dangerous?
6. Why is it important to know what the tide is doing at the seaside?
7. Why can it be dangerous to play with inflatable toys or air beds in the sea?
8. Why can swimming in a canal be dangerous?
9. Why should you not jump in to try to save someone?
10. How should you try to try to help if you see someone in difficulty in the water?

Note: ROSPA has details of the Water Code on its website, which you can use to check answers.

SPOT THE DANGERS (Years 3 and 4 drawing activity)

Invite the children in pairs or groups to produce a drawing on a large sheet of paper showing a scene which includes a river, a canal and a lake. Encourage them to include in the drawing as many hazards as they can. For example, they might show someone about to dive into the river from a bridge or someone trying to climb a steep bank out of a canal or someone being swept down a river by a strong current. Groups can swap their completed pictures with another group and try to spot all the hazards in the picture.

ACCIDENTS AND EMERGENCIES (Years 3 and 4 discussion)

Make a set of cards with one of these situations written on each:

- A friend falls in a river or canal.
- A friend falls off their skateboard and is knocked unconscious.
- You are cycling through a wood and are caught in a fierce thunderstorm.

- A friend falls awkwardly and you think they may have broken a bone.
- A friend cuts themselves badly.
- Someone falls in a frozen pond.
- A friend gets trapped in a cave.
- A friend gets stuck while climbing a cliff.
- You get stung by a wasp or bee.

Put the cards in a box and pass it round the circle. When you clap your hands the person who is holding the box takes out a card and reads it. The person then has to say what they would do in that situation. The rest of the class then discuss whether it's the right thing to do or not. Repeat the activity until all the cards have been drawn out of the box.

Point out that so long as a person's life is not in danger the most important thing to do is to get adult help.

FIREWORKS – BE SAFE, NOT SORRY (Years 4–6 discussion/ role play)

Aim: To emphasise the dangers of fireworks.

Introduce the topic by explaining that because fireworks are dangerous, there is a fireworks code giving guidelines for adults on how to have a safe fireworks party. Invite the children in groups to suggest what rules about fireworks the fireworks code should contain, then compare their suggestions with the code (below).

The fireworks code

Keep fireworks in a closed box.
Follow the instructions on each firework.
Light all fireworks at arm's length.
Stand well back.
Never go back to a lit firework.
Never put fireworks in your pocket.
Never throw fireworks.
Keep pets indoors.

Ask the children: What are the reasons for each piece of advice?

Encourage the children to role play a TV studio discussion in which people put forward their views on fireworks and whether the sale of fireworks ought to be more tightly controlled. The children could take on the following roles: a shopkeeper who sells fireworks, a parent of a child who has been injured in a fireworks accident, a fire officer, a representative from a firm that makes fireworks, a trading standards officer concerned about the sale of imported fireworks, an MP who wants tighter control of the manufacture and sale of fireworks, a teenager who has a blog, Fireworks Are Fun.

Invite the children to plan and produce a short radio or TV item designed to warn young people of the dangers of fooling around with fireworks.

Encourage the children in groups to role play a scene in which one of them thinks it would be fun to throw a firework into a garden where there is a pet dog or cat. Another one of the group encourages him to do so, thinking it would be a laugh while the other members of the group try to persuade him not to do it.

FIRST AID (Years 5–8 research/producing a leaflet or power point presentation)

Encourage the children in groups to use the internet to research how to give first aid and to produce a leaflet or a power point presentation on how to give basic first aid. Different members of the group can take responsibility for different injuries, such as cuts and grazes, suspected fractures, burns and scalds.

As a follow-up activity you can demonstrate to the children how to make a sling and how to put on a bandage.

You can also show them a first aid kit and discuss when and how to use the items it contains.

WHAT SHOULD YOU DO? (Years 3–6 discussion)

Discuss each of the situations in turn, asking the children what they think you should do if you are in that situation.

- You get lost while out playing.
- Someone jumps in front of you and blocks your way.
- You are alone at home and someone comes to the door.
- Someone offers you a treat if you will do something you don't want to do.
- It's pouring with rain and someone offers you a lift home in their car.
- You hurt yourself in the park and someone says they will take you to their house and put a bandage on your wound.
- You hear footsteps behind you and think someone is following you.
- You are waiting by a lift and someone you are not sure of comes to stand beside you.
- Someone meets you outside school and says your parents have asked them to take you home.
- An adult asks you to promise to keep something secret.

ONLINE SAFETY – RISKS AND CONSEQUENCES (Years 5–8 risks box)

Aim: To understand what are risky behaviours online and what the consequences may be.

Introduce the idea of a risks box. Ask the children in groups to think of what is risky behaviour when they are online, e.g. on social networking sites, and to write the different examples of risky behaviour on separate cards and to put them in the risks box.

Include in the box some examples that you have prepared, such as giving out personal information, posting online details of a party or when your family are going to be away for the weekend, sending rude messages, spreading rumours, downloading a video from a file-sharing website, meeting someone online and agreeing to meet them in person.

Pass the box around the class and ask children in turn to pick out one of the cards and discuss what the consequences of taking that risk might be.

SAFER SEX – MYTHS AND FACTS (Years 7 and 8 team activity)

Aim: To understand what are facts and myths about sex.

Make a set of statement cards, consisting of myths and facts about sex. Give a set of cards to each group and ask them to sort the cards into two piles – one of myths and one of facts (see the list below). Ask them to put a set of the cards into a box and draw them out one by one. Read the statement on the card and discuss whether it should go on the fact or myth pile. When they have finished, give the answers. If the group put the card onto the correct pile, they score one point. If they put it on the wrong pile, they lose a point. The winning group is the one with the most points at the end. Encourage the children to visit the NHS Choices website, www.nhs.uk where there are four 'Sex myth buster' interactive quizzes.

1. You can't get pregnant the first time you have sex.
2. Using a condom gives you protection against getting pregnant or catching an STI.
3. The best way to avoid getting an STI is to delay having sex until you are older and with a partner you can trust.
4. You can't get pregnant if your partner withdraws before ejaculation.
5. It is easy to tell if you have a sexually transmitted infection.
6. You are more likely to have unsafe sex if you've been drinking or taking drugs.
7. Only people who sleep around get themselves pregnant.
8. Movies and TV programmes give a realistic picture of sex.
9. When someone says No to having sex, they mean No.
10. You cannot get pregnant during your period.

11. You cannot get pregnant if you have sex standing up.
12. If you haven't got a condom, you can protect yourself by using clingfilm.
13. You can catch an STI from a toilet seat.
14. You can't get pregnant through having oral sex.
15. You can catch an STI from having a tattoo or body piercing.
16. You can catch an STI from having oral sex.
17. You don't need to use a condom if your partner is on the pill.
18. No form of contraception is 100% effective.
19. Two condoms are better than one.
20. If you wash yourself thoroughly after sex, you won't get pregnant.

Note: 1 Myth; 2 Fact; 3 Fact; 4 Myth; 5 Myth; 6 Fact; 7 Myth; 8 Myth; 9 Fact;10 Myth; 11 Myth; 12 Myth; 13 Myth; 14 Fact; 15 Fact; 16 Fact; 17 Myth; 18 Fact; 19 Myth; 20 Myth.

WHAT IS CHILD ABUSE? (Years 7 and 8 discussion)

Aim: To understand that child abuse may take several forms – physical, sexual, emotional or neglect.

Make copies of the list below and then ask children in groups to put a cross beside those actions which they consider to be child abuse, a question mark beside those actions they are unsure about and a tick beside those actions which they agree are acceptable behaviour. Then compare their views in a class discussion and point out that child abuse is not just physical and sexual, but may also take the form of neglect or emotional abuse.

- Punishing a child by locking them in their room
- Not allowing a child to watch TV after 9pm
- Forcing a child to take part in a sexual activity
- Forbidding a child to go outside to play
- Beating a child with a belt
- Preventing a child from getting medical treatment
- Neglecting to provide a child with enough food
- Threatening a child if they won't do what they are told

- Making a child watch pornography
- Constantly making sarcastic remarks about a child's behaviour
- Not allowing a child to celebrate their birthday or Christmas
- Slapping a child's face
- Not giving a child pocket-money
- Telling a child that they wish the child had never been born.

SMACKING – WHAT DO YOU THINK? (Years 5 and 6 studio discussion)

Invite the children in groups to role play a studio discussion on smacking as part of a television programme. The people taking part in the discussion are:

- Archibald Imallright who argues that smacking never did him any harm.
- Billy Beatenup who was frequently hit as a child and thinks smacking should be a crime.
- Sarah Unsure who is a mother of three and thinks that the occasional smack may be necessary.
- Charles Canem who thinks corporal punishment should be reintroduced and thinks smacking is a perfectly acceptable form of punishment.
- Lizzie Liberal who thinks there is no excuse for smacking a child.
- Tessa Tee-Vee presenter of the programme.

Encourage the children to prepare for the role play by using the internet to explore views on smacking and what the law is about smacking both in the UK and in other countries.

FACTS AND FICTIONS ABOUT SEXUAL ABUSE (Years 7 and 8 true or false quiz)

Aim: To understand some key facts about sexual abuse and to dispel some myths about sexual abuse.

Put the 10 statements below on the board and ask the children individually to say whether they are think they are true or false. Information about what is sexual abuse can be found on the Childline website – www.childline.org.uk

The answers are: 1 True, 2 False, 3 False, 4 True, 5 True, 6 True, 7 False, 8 False, 9 True, 10 True.

1. A young person is more likely to be abused by a person they know than by a stranger.
2. Child abuse only occurs in poor neighbourhoods.
3. Girls are more at risk than boys.
4. More than a third of children who are sexually abused by an adult do not report it.
5. The majority of offences are carried out by men.
6. Children who are sexually abused often feel guilty.
7. Abused children always grow up to become abusers as adults.
8. Victims are sometimes to blame for the abuse because of the way they behaved.
9. If anyone attempts to touch you in a way that makes you uncomfortable you have the right to tell them to stop.
10. You should always tell someone if you have been abused.

In a class discussion, point out that sexual abuse occurs in all neighbourhoods and in all parts of society; that boys are almost as much at risk as girls, though they report it less; that however provocatively an under-age person may have behaved it is always the adult who is responsible for the abuse and that although some abused children grow up to be abusers many do not.

WHAT IS SEXUAL HARASSMENT? (Years 7 and 8 ranking activity)

Aim: To understand what types of behaviour are sexual harassment.

Invite groups to define sexual harassment and to list examples of what they consider to be sexual harassment. Then compare their views in a class discussion. Prompt them, as necessary, to include the actions from the list below in their discussions. Finally ask them to rank the different actions on a scale of seriousness with 1 being the least serious and 10 the most serious. Discuss what stalking is and what you should do if you think you are being stalked.

- Deliberately bumping into someone in the corridor
- Following someone to their home
- Repeatedly asking someone to go out with you
- Making lewd remarks to members of the opposite sex
- Wolf-whistling
- Sending suggestive e-mails or text messages
- Taking someone's photo without their permission
- Commenting on someone's appearance
- Putting your arm round someone
- Teasing someone because of their sexuality.

SAFETY IN THE STREET: ASSESSING THE RISKS (Years 7 and 8 ranking activity)

Aim: To understand the different levels of risk in situations that may occur when young people are out and about.

Give groups a large sheet of paper and explain that you want them to make a RiskOmeter – a list of the level of risk involved in certain situations. The RiskOmeter has a scale of 1 to 10 – 1 being a low risk 5 a medium risk and 10 a high risk. Put the list of situations on the board and ask them where they would place them on the RiskOmeter. Encourage them to add other situations involving risk that they can think of and to include them on their RiskOmeter.

Compare their views in a class discussion and discuss what they would do in each situation.

- Missing the last bus home and being offered a lift home by someone you don't know
- Taking a shortcut down a deserted alleyway in the dark

- Travelling home alone on a bus in the evening after being at the cinema
- Waiting outside a cinema alone for a parent to pick you up
- Being approached by someone you don't know and asked for money
- Walking past a large group of football supporters
- Being offered a lift home by a friend's elder brother who has been drinking
- Walking past a group of older youths who start shouting and swearing at you
- Waiting at night on a railway platform
- Finding you haven't enough money left to pay for a bus or train home
- Being spoken to by someone you don't know in a toilet.

SAFETY IN THE STREET – TOP TIPS (Years 7 and 8 discussion and writing)

Aim: To consider the best ways to stay safe in the street.

Do a brainstorm and produce a spidergram of their ideas.

Keep to well-lit
streets

Wear a
reflective jacket

Don't walk closely
behind someone
who is alone

Make sure your
mobile is charged

If attacked,
shout FIRE

Don't lie about
where you are
going to be

**STREET
SAFETY**

Don't take shortcuts
down dark alleyways
or lanes

Don't walk alone
if you can avoid it

Don't accept lifts
from people you
don't know

Ignore anyone
who shouts at you

Discuss each piece of advice that is given and why it is important to follow it. Add any other suggestions that the children make, such as carry a torch if you are walking along places where it is dark. Talk about places that are not well-lit in your neighbourhood and discuss how it is safer to take a longer route down well-lit streets than to take a shortcut down a dark path.

Encourage groups to make a power point presentation of their top tips.

As a follow-up, you could invite your local community police officer to come in and discuss street safety with the class.

PART 3
Living in the wider world

CHAPTER 17

Your neighbours, your neighbourhood

The activities in this chapter focus on exploring the neighbourhoods in which the children live. There is the opportunity for them to discuss the places they can play, to survey the condition of the neighbourhood and how safe it is and to present plans for a new playground. There is also an activity on vandals and vandalism.

A NEIGHBOURHOOD SURVEY (Years 5 and 6 survey)

Aim: To survey the appearance and condition of the neighbourhood and how safe it is.

Ask the children in groups to carry out a survey of their neighbourhood in order to establish how safe it is and what its appearance is like. Encourage them to consider the following:

- Are the roads in good repair? Are there speed limits on any of the roads? Are there safe places to cross? Are there cycle lanes?
- Are the pavements safe or do they need repairing? Are the streets safe at night? Are they well enough lit?
- Are any parks or playgrounds well maintained and safe? Is any playground equipment in good condition? Are play areas fenced off? Are they free of dog's excreta?
- Is the neighbourhood clean and free of litter? Are there any places where people have just dumped rubbish or old vehicles? Is there any graffiti or vandalism?
- Are there any streams, rivers or lakes? Are they clean or polluted?

Ask groups to report their findings to the rest of the class. Then invite them to draft a letter to send to the local council stating what they think needs to be done to improve the neighbourhood or congratulating the council on how well it is looking after the neighbourhood.

PLACES TO PLAY (Years 3–6 discussion/role play)

Aim: To discuss places where children play

Lead a class discussion of places they used to play in when they were smaller and places they like to play now. Ask: What makes them good places to play? Encourage them to think about each of the places. Ask: Do adults object to children playing there and, if so, why? Prompt them to think about concerns such as whether someone might get hurt, whether they might cause damage, whether they might be a nuisance, whether it might be dangerous.

Ask them to choose one of the places they talked about in their groups. Invite them to role play a scene in which an adult explains to a child why they object to them playing in a particular place. Alternatively, act out a scene in which a young person gets injured, while playing in an area that adults had warned them was dangerous.

A NEW PLAY AREA (Years 5–8 planning a presentation)

Aim: To design a new play area

Ask the children to imagine that the local council is planning to build a new play area in a local park or an area of waste ground. It is running a competition for children in which they have to design the new play area.

Invite groups to choose a suitable site in the neighbourhood (e.g. an old play area that needs updating) and to draw a plan and to

111

discuss what equipment they would like to have. Prompt them to consider such things as:

1. Safety. They will need to ensure that there are soft surfaces to land and to consider such things as whether the area needs to be fenced off.
2. They need to think of the needs of people with disabilities.
3. They need to think of the environment. The design needs to fit in with the existing environment and not be an eyesore.

Invite the children to give their presentations. Discuss how they could prepare a leaflet illustrating their plan or they could do a power point presentation. You could invite a local councillor to judge their presentations and to choose a winner.

VANDALISM – WHAT DO YOU THINK? (Years 5 and 6 discussion/role play)

Aim: To explore the problem of vandalism.

Introduce the topic of vandalism by asking the children what the term vandalism means and make a list on the board of examples they give of vandalism. Then put the poem below on the board and ask them to discuss why Victor is a vandal. Ask: Why might he feel so angry that he goes round committing acts of vandalism? Talk about why young people get involved in vandalism. Prompt the children to consider points such as boredom, jealousy and frustration.

Focus on the different acts of vandalism Victor commits. Encourage groups to discuss whether some are more serious than others. Ask what their attitude to graffiti is. Does it depend on where the graffiti is written?

Invite pairs to act out a scene in which an adult who has caught a young person committing an act of vandalism tells them off and explains why it is a serious matter.

Then ask the pairs to imagine that they have to decide what punishment to give to a young person who has been found guilty of an act of vandalism that has caused someone to have an accident.

Victor the vandal

I'm Victor. I'm a vandal
And I really do not care.
With my spray can in my hand
I squirt graffiti everywhere.

I kick all the litter bins
As I walk down the street
And when I'm on a bus
I pull the stuffing from the seat.

I go into empty houses
I break the locks on doors.
I throw bricks through the windows.
I pull boards up from the floors.

I stomp into allotments
I rip planks from gardeners' sheds
I break branches off the trees
And trample flower beds.

I'm Victor. I'm a vandal
And I really do not care
With my spray can in my hand
I leave my anger everywhere.

CHAPTER 18
Rules and responsibilities

This chapter focuses on the reasons why we have rules and explains that wherever there are rules there are accompanying responsibilities. There is an activity on the country code. It also contains activities on stealing, the rules the children would make for a new school and those that they would make for a group who were stranded on a deserted island.

THE COUNTRYSIDE CODE (Years 3–6 discussion/writing)

Aim: To understand that it is important to look after the countryside.

Explain to the children that when they are out playing or walking in the countryside they need to behave responsibly and that there is a countryside code which they should follow. Ask them to make a list of rules which they think should be included in the countryside code.

Then share their lists in a class discussion. Put the rules that they suggest on the board, then show them the list (below) and prompt them to add any rules from it that are not on their list of suggestions. A leaflet giving full details of the countryside code can be downloaded at www.gov.uk

- Always close gates.
- Stick to paths.
- Don't walk through fields of wheat or hay.
- Keep your dog on a lead.
- When riding a bike slow down or stop for horse riders and farm animals.

- Do not chase wild animals.
- Do not uproot plants or break branches off trees.
- Take your litter home.
- Don't throw uneaten food away.
- Don't leave broken bottles lying around.
- Don't climb over fences, walls or hedges.
- Don't play with farm machinery
- Don't play near pylons.
- Don't trespass on private property.

Ask the children to discuss each of the rules in turn and to suggest what the consequences might be if they ignored these rules. Then encourage them in groups to act out a scene in which a farmer gets angry with a group of children because they have failed to follow one or more of the rules.

DEALING WITH STEALING (Years 6 and 7 role play)

Aim: To explore attitudes to stealing.

Act out a studio discussion in a TV programme called 'Have your say' in which a panel of experts share their views on what an adult should do if a young person is caught stealing. The panellists should include people with different views. You can either get the panellists to decide for themselves what their views are going to be or give them one of the following viewpoint cards:

'Young thieves should be made to meet their victims and apologise.'

'It depends on the value of the item they stole. If it's only a packet of crisps or a bar of chocolate they should just get a ticking off.'

'We're too soft these days. They should be given a clip round the ear.'

'They need to be dealt with by the police.'

'It depends on whether it's their first offence.'

YOUR RIGHTS AT SCHOOL (Years 5 and 6 a ranking activity/ discussion)

Aim: To discuss what rights children have at school.

Invite the children in groups to draw up a list of their rights at school and to rank them according to how important they think each right is *****extremely important ***very important *important.

Encourage them to think about such rights as to be spoken to politely and treated with respect, to be able to work without being disturbed or distracted, to move round the school without being bullied or harassed, to have classrooms that are clean, heated and well ventilated, to have clean and hygienic changing rooms and toilets, to have a safe place to store possessions.

Raise the question of whether they have these rights: a right to a break-time, a right to have a playground, a right to have something to eat when they feel hungry, a right to sit next to whoever they choose.

Get the children to share their lists in a class discussion. Then point out that having rights also means that you have a responsibility to respect the rights of others. For example, if you consider it is your right to have a clean classroom, it is your responsibility to keep it tidy, not to drop litter and not to damage the furniture.

Draw two columns on a large sheet of paper and list the rights they have at school and the responsibilities they have as a result.

THE UNIFORM QUESTION (Years 6–8 a debate)

Aim: To debate the issue of whether a school should have a uniform.

Read out this statement and ask the children to indicate by a show of hands whether they agree or disagree with it: 'Schoolchildren should have the right to wear what they like to school'. Then ask the children why they agree or disagree with this view.

Ask the children: Why do most schools have a uniform? Encourage them to research adults' opinions on uniform to find out what parents and teachers think.

Then hold a debate on the motion, 'Children should not be forced to wear a uniform to school'.

SCHOOL RULES OK? (Years 3–6 discussion)

Aim: To discuss what rules a school should have.

Invite the children to imagine that a new school is to be opened and that the school council has been asked by the headteacher to draw up a set of school rules. Ask groups to hold a meeting of the school council at which they discuss and decide what rules they would have. Get them to write the rules on a large sheet of paper and to choose a member of the group to explain what rules your school will have and why.

Put the following questions on the board as prompts:

What rules will you have about ... uniform, jewellery and make-up?
behaviour in the classroom?
behaviour round the school?
items that can be brought into school?
absence from school?
leaving the school premises?

In a class discussion, ask the class to agree on a set of rules for the new school and then ask them to discuss the relative importance of each of the rules and to rank the rules in order of importance.

Invite groups to decide what punishments, if any, they would give to a person for breaking a particular rule. Share their ideas about punishments in a class discussion and draw out the idea that the main purpose of any punishment should not be to take revenge on a person for doing something wrong, but to make the individual think about what they have done, to get them to understand why it is wrong and to make sure that they do not do the same thing again.

As a follow-up, you can get the groups to role play a scene in which someone breaks a school rule and is punished for doing so. In the debriefing, discuss whether the punishment was fair or not.

WHAT RULES WOULD YOU MAKE? (Years 5–8 discussion)

Aim: To discuss the rules they would make if they were stranded on a desert island.

Invite the children to imagine there has been a disaster which has killed everyone in the world except a small group of them who have survived because they happened to be visiting a remote island at the time. There are no adults left alive as the teachers who were with them went to seek help and never returned. Encourage them to hold a meeting at which they discuss what rules they are going to make about living on the island and who is going to make the decisions on the island.

CHAPTER 19
Values and beliefs

In this chapter there are activities which explore children's attitudes to what is acceptable and unacceptable behaviour, to stealing and cheating, and to violence and fighting. Other activities focus on people they admire and what characteristics heroes have. There is also an activity focusing on religious beliefs and activities which explore the subject of gambling.

YOUR VALUES: RIGHT AND WRONG (Years 5–7 ranking activity)

Aim: To discuss the level of seriousness of certain actions.

Put theses sentences on the board and ask the children individually to complete the statements, saying how serious they think each type of behaviour is – extremely serious, very serious, serious or not very serious and to give the reasons for their view. Then invite them to compare and discuss their opinions in groups, before sharing them in a class discussion.

1. I think painting graffiti on a neighbour's wall is…
2. I think stealing a magazine from a newsagent's is…
3. I think playing truant from school is…
4. I think punching someone in the face is…
5. I think swearing at an old lady is…
6. I think throwing empty bottles and food cartons out of a car window is…
7. I think hitting a stray cat with a stick is…
8. I think riding on a bus without a ticket is…
9. I think bullying someone by making hurtful remarks about their weight is…

10. I think blackmailing someone by threatening to reveal a secret about them unless they pay you not to do so is…
11. I think letting someone else take the blame for something you did is…
12. I think taking someone's bicycle and riding it without their permission is…

THE DARE (Years 5 and 6 role play/discussion)

Aim: To consider the consequences of agreeing to do a dare.

In groups of four ask the children to role play a scene in which a boy or girl called Sam is dared by another boy or girl to steal a bar of chocolate from a corner shop. Sam is spotted doing so by a customer who tells the shopkeeper and wants to call the police. Another customer becomes involved in the discussion about what action should be taken.

You can make character cards to give the children to help them with their roles.

SAM: Basically honest. Has never done anything like this before but seeks Pat's approval and wants to be friends with Pat. Is very concerned about taking something from the shopkeeper as he does a paper round for him.

SHOPKEEPER: Likes Sam as he is a reliable paper boy. Can't understand why he would do such a thing. Wants to give Sam a telling off but doesn't want to involve the police.

CUSTOMER A: Is outraged by Sam's behaviour. Thinks he should be taught a lesson. Wants to call the police on her mobile.

CUSTOMER B: Knows Sam and his parents. Thinks they will be horrified, especially if the police are involved. Becomes involved in the discussion about what should be done.

Take it in turns to show your role plays to the class and to discuss the different outcomes.

Hold a discussion of the view that it can take more courage to refuse a dare than to accept it.

CHEATING (Years 5–6 discussion)

Aim: To discuss views about cheating.

Put the statements (below) on the board and invite the children to discuss them, before sharing their views in a class discussion.

- It is OK to ask a friend for help with your homework.
- It is OK if your parent does your homework for you.
- Using the internet to find out the answers to your homework is not cheating.
- Copying a friend's homework word-for-word is cheating.
- Helping a friend with answers to a test is cheating.
- Anyone who cheats in an exam should be automatically disqualified.
- Cheating is all right so long as you don't get caught.
- People who cheat at sports should be banned from playing.

VIOLENCE (Years 5–8 discussion)

Aim: To explore attitudes to violence.

Put the statements below on the board and ask the children in groups to discuss each statement in turn and to say whether they agree or disagree with it.

- If someone hits you, you should hit them back.
- Boxing should be banned.
- TV programmes and films glamorise violence.
- You should never hit a woman.
- You should only use violence in self-defence.
- If you see someone being attacked, you shouldn't intervene.
- Sportsmen guilty of violent behaviour during a game should be prosecuted.

- Corporal punishment should be allowed in schools.
- Smacking children is a form of child abuse.
- There is too much violence in computer games.

Focus on violence in TV programmes and films. Record an advert for a forthcoming film which is either a crime, gangster or war movie. Ask them to observe which of the following behaviours it contains: yelling, swearing, threatening, bullying, punching, shooting, killing, bombing, torturing.

Ask: Do you think violence in TV and films causes you to have a distorted view of the atrocities you see on news bulletins? Do you think it makes people more aggressive?

RELIGIOUS BELIEFS AND VALUES (Years 5–7 research/ discussion)

Aim: To understand that people's values and beliefs are often determined by their religions.

Explain that many people's values and beliefs are based on what religious group they belong to. Encourage the children to research the rules about eating certain foods that there are in certain religions. Ask them to try to find out why these foods are not allowed by different religions.

Similarly, encourage them to research different customs about the clothes and religious symbols that people wear. Then talk about the laws there are in some societies forbidding the wearing of certain clothes in public. You can focus on the law in France which forbids the wearing of religious symbols in schools. What are the arguments for and against introducing such a ban in Britain?

HEROES – WHO DO YOU ADMIRE? (Years 6–8 discussion)

Aim: To discuss the reasons we admire people as heroes.

Introduce the topic by explaining that who we admire and regard as heroes will depend on what qualities we admire.

Put these statements on the board. Ask groups to discuss which of the people described they consider to be heroes. Then ask them individually to write down the name of one person who they would choose as their top hero.

> Someone who is willing to sacrifice their own life in order to save someone else's life, like the soldiers who are awarded the Victoria Cross.
>
> A person who is very talented and very dedicated and who makes the most of their ability to become successful, for example, an athlete like Mo Farah.
>
> Someone who makes a stand against injustice, even if it means they are imprisoned or put under house arrest, like Nelson Mandela.
>
> A person who makes a discovery that is of benefit to the whole of mankind, like Albert Einstein.
>
> People who put up with things and stay cheerful and overcome adversity to achieve, like the disabled athlete Tanni Grey-Thompson.
>
> People who refuse to accept defeat and keep on campaigning even when things go against them, like Stephen Lawrence's mother.
>
> People who have done something courageous like rowed across the Atlantic or swum the Channel.
>
> People who have shown enormous bravery, for example, by going into a blazing building to rescue someone who is trapped.
>
> Sports stars, pop stars and film stars, who make good role models, are a type of hero.
>
> My cousin who lost both his legs in Afghanistan and who walked to the South Pole.
>
> Someone who dedicates their life to looking after people less fortunate than themselves, such as Mother Teresa.

WHAT QUALITIES DO HEROES HAVE? (Years 6–8 discussion)

Aim: To consider what qualities heroes have.

Ask the children to discuss and make a list of the qualities that they think heroes have. Give them an example of a quality they might include, such as unselfishness. Get them to share their lists in a class discussion. Below is a list of qualities that you might introduce into the discussion. Can the class agree on what they think are the most important qualities?

> dedication, courage, tolerance, tact, determination, unselfishness, generosity, cheerfulness, kindness, sympathy, patience, intelligence, perseverance, honesty, compassion

HEROES – WHO WOULD YOU SAVE? (Years 6–8 balloon debate)

Aim: To compare and judge the qualities of different heroes.

Put the names of a number of famous people in a box. Imagine that these people are on board a ship which is sinking. A helicopter arrives in time to winch one of them to safety. Invite them in turn to give the reasons why they think their hero should be saved. When everyone has stated their reasons, each person in the class writes down the name of the person they think should be saved.

Note: They cannot vote for their own hero.

Encourage the groups to choose one person as their hero of heroes and get a reporter to explain their reasons to the rest of the class. Hold a vote to choose one person to go into the heroes hall of fame.

I WOULD LIKE TO … (Years 5–7 writing/discussion)

Aim: To think about what they would like to do in the future and what this tells them about their values.

Ask the children what things they would like to do when they are older. For example, to travel round the world, to go to university, to earn lots of money, to get married and have a family, to have a job that they enjoy, to do something that will help other people, to become a celebrity, to be an international sports star, to go into space, to be happy, to have a nice house, to own an expensive car. Ask them to make a list in order of importance of at least three things they would like to do as adults. Invite them to share their lists and explain their reasons for their ideas. Then, as a class, discuss how what they chose to put on their lists says about what their values are.

IT ISN'T RIGHT TO FIGHT (Years 7 and 8 discussion)

Aim: To explore attitudes to war and fighting.

Use this poem to introduce the topic of wars and fighting.

It isn't right to fight

You said, 'It isn't right to fight,'
But when we watched the news tonight,
You shook your fist and said
You wished the tyrant and his cronies dead.
When I asked why,
If it's not right to fight,
You gave a sigh,
You shook your head
And sadly said,
'Sometimes a cause is just
And, if there is no other way,
Perhaps, you must.'

Hold a class discussion. Ask the children: If your country went to war, would you volunteer to join the forces? Would it depend on whether an enemy was attacking your country or whether the war was to defend another country?

Explain what conscription is. Ask: If the government passes a law saying that everyone aged 18–25 must join the forces would you join up or refuse to go? Would it make a difference if you were a married man or married woman with two children? What if your religion told you it was wrong to go to war and kill people? Would you be prepared to take a non-combatant role or to go to prison? What is your view of people who were conscientious objectors in the First and Second World Wars?

DEALING WITH CONFLICT (Years 7 and 8 discussion)

Aim: To explore ways of dealing with conflict.

Invite the children to discuss what they should do in the situations below. Ask: Is it their duty to intervene? What should they do, if anything? Would they behave differently in the two situations? Discuss the view that it's better to do nothing than to intervene.

Imagine they decide to say something. Ask groups to decide what would be the best thing to say and what would be the worst.

Situation A: You are standing waiting to cross the road. A car pulls in and another car screeches to a halt beside it. The driver of the second car leaps out and starts shouting and swearing at the other driver and grabs him by the collar. There is no else about.

Situation B: You are sitting in a railway carriage when a crowd of football fans pours in and starts taunting an opposition supporter. It looks as though things might get out of hand unless you do something.

YOUR VALUES – GAMBLING: WHAT DO YOU THINK? (Years 7 and 8 discussion)

Aim: To explore attitudes to gambling.

Explain that gambling is not allowed in some religions and discuss the reasons why.

Ask: What is your attitude to gambling? Do you think it is a mug's game or just harmless fun? Should gambling be banned, as it is in some countries? Are people who oppose gambling just killjoys?

End the discussion by holding a vote to see if they think it is true that gambling causes more harm and distress than it gives pleasure.

WHY DO PEOPLE GAMBLE? (Years 6–8 discussion)

Aim: To explore the reasons why people gamble.

Encourage individuals to write down the reasons why people gamble, then to share their views in a group discussion, before sharing them with the rest of the class.

Points made in the class discussion should include: excitement – the thrill of waiting to see if you've won; it's glamorous – you see people in films gambling in casinos and you see celebrities gambling; people gamble in the hope of winning enough to make their dreams come true; it's a way of escaping problems such as boredom; your peers pressurise you; you don't want to be thought a killjoy.

WHAT IS RESPONSIBLE GAMBLING? (Years 6–8 a writing activity)

Aim: To understand what responsible gambling means.

Explain that responsible gambling means making sure that gambling does not take over your life.

Put these top tips for responsible gambling on the board and ask the class to pick out the three pieces of advice they think to be the most important and to give their reasons.

• Never gamble with money you can't afford to lose.

- Set a limit on the amount of money you plan to gamble with.
- Don't regard gambling as a way to make money.
- If you have a lucky streak, quit while you are ahead.
- Set a time limit on how long you are going to gamble and stick to it.
- Don't drink and gamble. You are more likely to gamble more than you can afford if you have been drinking.
- Don't gamble in order to try to impress other people.
- Don't spend too much of your leisure time gambling. Make sure you do other activities too.
- Don't let gambling take over your life. If it's becoming a problem, talk to someone about your worries.

Then, invite individuals to write a reply to Sam's letter to Dear Dorothy (below).

> Dear Dorothy
>
> I enjoy gambling, but I don't want to become addicted to it. How can I ensure that I don't let gambling take over my life? I've heard people talking about responsible gambling. What do they mean? Sam

Invite the children to role play a conversation between two friends in which one of them tries to persuade the other to stop gambling because it is having such a bad effect on their life.

A NEW SUPER CASINO (Years 7 and 8 role play)

Aim: To debate the arguments for and against the building of a new super casino.

Invite the class to imagine that a planning application has been made to build a new super casino in the town where you live. Discuss what arguments people might put forward in favour and against the proposal and list the ideas they suggest on the board. Decide who the people might be who would be in favour of the casino being built and who would be against. Then act out an open meeting at which the different views are expressed, before inviting the class to vote for or against the proposal.

CHAPTER 20

Prejudice, stereotyping and discrimination

The activities in this chapter explore what is meant by stereotyping, focusing on issues of gender stereotyping, prejudice and racism and ageism. There are also activities about attitudes towards immigrants.

THE SAME, ONLY DIFFERENT (Years 3 and 4 a circle game)

Aim: To understand similarities and differences between people.

Prepare for this game by getting the children to cut out pictures from magazines and newspapers of children from all over the world. Then ask them to choose one of the pictures, and to stick a picture or drawing of that child's face onto a piece of cardboard and to fix the cardboard face to a stick.

Ask them to think about how that child is similar to them and how the child is different from them. Go round the circle and ask them in turn to hold up the child's face and to state one way that the child is similar to them and one way that the child is different from them. If any of them find it difficult, ask other members of the group to suggest things they could say. After you have been round the circle, ask them what we can learn from this exercise and point out that however different we may look and however different our lives we are all human beings with similar feelings and needs.

THE LINE (Years 5 and 6 whole class activity)

Aim: To illustrate that we cannot judge what people are like by their physical appearance.

The aim of this game is to demonstrate that it is impossible to base your image of people on their physical characteristics, appearance, dress or some other factor, such as their date of birth.

Tell the children to imagine that they live in a society in which only certain people are eligible for the ruling class and that the others are considered to be fit only to be workers.

Then ask the children to line up with, for example, those wearing spectacles at the back and everyone else at the front.

Explain that in the society all people wearing spectacles are considered to be too intellectual to be worth considering for the ruling class. They are to sit down.

Now ask the remaining children what colour their hair is. All children with fair hair must go at the back. They are considered to be too artistic to be members of the ruling class and must sit down.

Ask the remaining children what colour socks they have on. All children with white socks are to go at the back of the line. They are considered to be too ambitious to be members of the ruling class and must sit down.

Continue the activity until either only one or two are left in the line or all the children have been excluded from the ruling class.

Other things that could be used to place children at the back of the line are:

- Those whose birthdays are in the first six months of the year.
- Those who have a baby brother or sister under the age of five.
- Those who have green eyes.
- Those who have packed lunches.

Then hold a class discussion about what the game teaches you about stereotyping.

HOW CAN YOU TELL WHAT A PERSON IS LIKE? (Years 5 and 6 discussion)

Aim: To discuss how we can judge what people are like.

For this activity you need to prepare sets of statement cards to give to each group. The children then have to sort the cards into three piles, according to whether they agree or disagree with the statement. The third pile is for any statement they are not sure about. When they have sorted the cards, ask them to share their views in a class discussion.

The cards have the following statements suggesting how you can tell what a person is like:

By the way they speak	By what sort of house they live in
By their sense of humour	By how they treat animals
By the colour of their skin	By how much you can trust them
By how many friends they have	By what their religion is
By their haircut	By what makes them angry
By their size and shape	By how generous they are
By what nationality they are	By the clothes they wear
By how confident they are	By how good at sports they are
By how selfish they are	

DO YOU STEREOTYPE PEOPLE? (Years 5 and 6 discussion)

Aim: To consider how people are stereotyped.

Put the following statements on the board. All of the statements are statements that stereotype people.

1. Everyone from the West Indies likes cricket and reggae.
2. All Scotsmen wear kilts and like highland dancing.
3. People with red hair are more quick-tempered than other people.
4. People who are left-handed are more artistic than right-handed people.
5. Men are better at handling money than women.
6. All old people are forgetful.
7. All people from London are snobs.
8. French people are better chefs than English people.

Ask individuals to write down whether they agree or disagree with the statements before sharing their answers in groups and as a class. Conclude with a discussion of what they have learned about stereotyping from this activity.

GENDER STEREOTYPING (Years 7 and 8 discussion)

Aim: To explore gender stereotyping.

Introduce the topic by explaining what stereotyping means: having an image of a group of people which ignores the differences within that group.

Ask the children to draw two columns on a piece of paper, one labelled man, the other labelled woman and then to list the characteristics that are often attributed to them. For example, under man they might put 'tough', under woman they might put 'good with children'.

When they have drawn up their lists, share the characteristics they have identified in a class discussion by putting them into two columns on the board.

Points that might be included are: Man – aggressive, tough, breadwinner, practical, strong, good at science and maths, sporty, doesn't cry, leader, big, beer-drinker. Woman – soft, gentle, homemaker, cries easily, good with children, sensitive, multi-tasker, supportive.

Ask them whether the list give an accurate description. Do the characteristics describe all men and all women? Talk about how they are stereotypes and how it isn't possible to make a statement such as 'All men are practical'. End with a discussion of what they have learned from the activity about gender stereotyping.

MEN'S JOBS, WOMEN'S JOBS (Years 5–6 discussion)

Aim: To understand that there are no such things as men's jobs and women's jobs.

Invite the children in groups to discuss each of the statements below in turn, saying why they agree or disagree with them.

- Some jobs are not suitable for women.
- The best jobs for women are ones that allow them to be at home when their children are.
- Women make better secretaries than men.
- Women aren't strong enough to do jobs like bricklaying.
- Engineering is not a good career choice for girls.
- Women are less good at practical jobs than men.
- Men are the main breadwinners, so it's right that they are paid more.
- There's a good reason why there aren't more women in top management posts. It's because they aren't as tough as men.
- All firms should allow women to work flexible hours.
- Companies should be made to interview at least one woman candidate when they have a job vacancy.

WHAT'S IN A NAME? (Years 5–6 discussion)

Aim: To recognise how older people are often stereotyped.

Introduce the activity by talking about nicknames and how hurtful nicknames can be. Then ask the children in groups to list as many words or phrases as they can which are used to describe older people e.g. pensioners, senior citizens. Ask them to include slang terms, such as wrinklies, has-beens.

Compile a class list on the board. Other names which might be included are: the elderly, geriatrics, old crocks, old fogies, biddies, buffers, golden oldies, old codgers, grannies, over the hill, ancients, old dears. Discuss how many of the terms are negative ones. Ask: if you were aged over 75, which of the terms would you prefer people to use? Which would you find insulting?

As a follow-up, the children can ask relatives, such as great-grand-parents, which words they prefer people to use when talking about people of their age.

WHAT IS YOUR ATTITUDE TO OLDER PEOPLE? (Years 5–8 discussion)

Aim: To explore attitudes towards older people.

Put the statements below on the board and ask groups to discuss each one in turn, explaining why they agree or disagree with it. Then hold a class discussion in which they share their views.

- Older people deserve our pity because they have poor memories.
- Older people shouldn't expect to rely on the state to look after them.
- Older people should not be given expensive medical treatment.
- Older people should allow relatives to make decisions for them.
- Older people should be forced to retire at 70.
- Older people should not get free prescriptions if they can afford to pay for them.
- Older people over the age of 70 should not be able to drive.
- Older people should not get the state pension if they are rich.
- Older people should not live on their own if they cannot look after themselves.
- Families should be made to take responsibility for elderly relatives.

WHAT IS YOUR VIEW OF IMMIGRANTS? (Years 7 and 8 discussion)

Aim: To explore attitudes towards immigrants and immigration.

Put the statements (below) on the board, then discuss each one in turn, asking for a show of hands to indicate whether not they agree or disagree with the statement and to give reasons for their opinion.

- Immigrants have contributed a great deal to British society.
- There are too many immigrants.
- Immigrants often take jobs that British people are unwilling to do.
- Immigrants come to Britain because they can scrounge off the state.
- We should only allow immigrants into Britain who are political refugees.
- Immigrants are responsible for the high crime rate in our cities.
- People who oppose immigration are racist.
- We should feel proud that people want to come to Britain, because it is a fair and just society.
- We should be able to deport any immigrants found guilty of a criminal offence*.
- Immigrants should have to pay for treatment in the NHS until they become British citizens.

Having discussed their views, go through the statements again and decide whether any of them are an expression of prejudice against immigrants.

*Note: Britain cannot deport criminals if the courts decide it would be a breach of their human rights (e.g. the right to a family life) to deport them.

NEWSWATCH (Years 7–8 research/discussion)

Aim: To identify examples of negative stereotyping.

Explain that newspaper headlines and news reports can stereo-type people by the language they use. Encourage the children to be on the lookout for headlines that are examples of racial stereo-typing and gender stereotyping or other types of stereotyping, such as stereotyping of teenagers, older people or immigrants. Get them to look through old newspapers and to cut out any stereo-typed headlines they find. Discuss what attitudes they suggest the headline writers have. Ask: Are they based on facts or opinions? Do they present a fair or unfair picture? They can then glue them on a poster and write comments saying whether they think the headlines present a true picture.

CHAPTER 21
Human rights

This unit contains activities to make children aware of what human rights are, to consider what rights children and parents have, to discuss violations of human rights and to comment on current human rights issues, including a debate on whether the death penalty should be introduced for convicted terrorists.

CHILDREN'S RIGHTS (Years 3–6 a ranking activity)

Aim: To understand what rights children have.

Brainstorm children's rights and produce a spidergram (see below).

The right to health and health care

The right to play

The right to an education

The right to life

The right to protection from harm

The right to a home

The right to a name and nationality

CHILDREN'S RIGHTS

The right to freedom of thought

The right to express their opinions

The right to enjoy their own culture

The right to live in peace

The right to an adequate standard of living

Ask groups to make a set of cards, each of which has one of the children's rights written on it. The groups' task is to rank the rights in order of importance from 1 to 12, then to compare their views in a class discussion.

WHAT'S MY RIGHT? (Years 5 and 6 team game)

Aim: To understand what are human rights.

Discuss what human rights are and draw a spidergram.

The list of rights should include:

The right
to life

The right to a
nationality

The right
to health

The right to
an education

The right to
privacy

The right
to vote

The right
to work

The right to
express your
opinions

**HUMAN
RIGHTS**

The right to
practice a religion

The right to a
fair trial

Freedom from
discrimination

Freedom
from slavery

Freedom of
association

The right to
own property

The right to marry
and have a family

Then to prepare for this activity you will need to produce a set of cards on which you have written each of the basic rights which we have as human beings (see page 138). Explain that this is a game in which groups compete against each other and get them to form teams of five or six and to choose a name for their group e.g The Know-It-Alls, the SuperRights.

Put the cards in a box and explain that you are going to choose people at random to pick a card on which is written a human right. The person then has to draw something which represents that right. The other members of the class have to guess what the right is. Whichever team guesses correctly gains a point.

HUMAN RIGHTS –WHAT DO YOU THINK? (Years 7 and 8 discussion)

Aim: To share views on issues concerning human rights.

Put the statements about human rights on the board and encourage the children in groups to say whether they agree or disagree with them, before sharing their views in a class discussion.

- We should intervene if we know people are being denied their rights by dictators.
- Censorship of the internet is a violation of human rights.
- Countries have the right to decide for themselves what are human rights.
- There should be sanctions against governments which deny people human rights.
- There's nothing we can do about human rights abuses. It's up to the governments to take action.
- Convicted criminals have the same human rights as everyone else.
- There are some circumstances in which using torture can be justified.

THE POLITICAL PRISONER (Years 5–6 discussion/writing)

Introduce the following scenario to the class: A reporter called James Liberty who wrote an article criticising the government of the dictator General Thug has disappeared. On the day the article appeared, the offices of his newspaper were ransacked by masked men. James was not in the office at the time, but he failed to return home that night. No one knows where he is. He is rumoured to be being held in the notorious Doomsday prison, where opponents of the government are known to have been tortured. It is six months since he disappeared.

Invite the children in groups to discuss which of James Liberty's human rights are being denied him and to draft an open letter to General Thug expressing their concern and demanding his immediate release.

VIOLATIONS OF HUMAN RIGHTS (Years 7–8 discussion)

Aim: To discuss a number of situations involving human rights issues.

Put the list of situations on the board and ask groups to discuss each situation in turn and to decide whether or not it is a violation of human rights and then to share their views in a class discussion.

1. A pupil is not allowed to wear the burkha in school.
2. A child goes to bed without any supper because her parents have no food to give her.
3. A parent reads a child's diary.
4. A parent refuses to send his children to school and says he is going to educate them at home.
5. A child is kept out of a sex education lesson for religious reasons.
6. A man who has a wife and family in Britain is deported because he has been found guilty of a serious crime.
7. The parents of a child refuse to give their consent to an operation that doctors say the child needs.

8. A person who wants to have an assisted suicide is prevented from travelling abroad to go to a clinic.
9. The police break up a demonstration because they are concerned about the safety of the demonstrators.
10. A person is threatened before they cast their vote in a referendum.

NEWSWATCH (Years 6–8 research/discussion)

Aim: To learn about current human rights issues.

Encourage the children to bring in copies of old newspapers and magazines and to look through them to find reports and stories that deal with human rights issues. Ask them to tell the class about any stories they find and invite them to comment on it. They can cut out any articles they find and put them on a news wall together with their comments.

YOUR RIGHTS AND YOUR PARENTS' RIGHTS (Years 5–6 discussion)

Ask the children to discuss what rights they have at home and what rights their parents have.

Put the list of statements about parents' rights on the board. Ask them whether they agree with the statements and to give their reasons.

Parents have the right:

- to choose which school you go to
- to smack you
- to choose whether to give you pocket money
- to make you do chores
- to choose what clothes you wear
- to choose your friends for you
- to make medical decisions for you

- to lock you in your room
- to decide who you live with
- to decide which DVDs you watch
- to decide which computer games you can play
- to decide when you have to go to bed.

AT WHAT AGE? (Years 5–6 discussion/writing)

Aim: To consider the ages at which children are allowed by law to do things.

Explain that there are laws about what children can do at certain ages. Encourage the children to use a black pen to draw a chart showing the ages at which they are allowed by law to do such things as drink alcohol, buy tobacco, get a part-time job, watch all kinds of films, vote, own a pet, buy a lottery ticket, join the army, drive a car, open a bank account, be held responsible for a crime. Encourage them to suggest any changes they think should be made to the laws and to use a red pen to write in any changes they would make to the ages.

THE RIGHTS OF PEOPLE WITH DISABILITIES (Years 3–6 discussion)

Aim: To explore what life is like for people with disabilities.

Introduce the topic of disability by asking the children to think of anyone they know who has a disability and make a list on the board of the different types of disability. Discuss how some people are born with a disability and how others become disabled through illness or an accident.

Ask them in pairs to imagine how their lives would be different if they had a physical disability. Think about the things that would be different if they couldn't move their legs or control their arms and legs properly. Ask: What would you find difficult to do? Make a list of activities you would find difficult.

Prompt them to include everyday activities such as getting dressed and undressed, washing and going to the toilet, moving round the house, reaching up for items on shelves, bending down to pick things up, travelling to school, playing sports.

Compare their lists in a class discussion. Then ask them what would not change about their lives if they had a disability. Discuss how they would still be themselves. They would still want to go out with their families, go to the cinema or to football matches, make friends and play with them, go to school and go away on holiday.

Focus on the rights of disabled people. Ask: How easy is it for people with disabilities to use public transport, to use the pavements and to gain access to buildings, such as shops, cinemas, sports arenas and cafes in your area? Are the needs of disabled people being met?

Encourage individuals to interview a disabled person and to report to the rest of the class what the disabled person said.

THE GREAT DEBATE (Years 7 and 8 debate)

Aim: To debate the issue of whether the death penalty should be reintroduced.

Ask the children to imagine that a bill has been introduced into Parliament proposing the reintroduction of the death penalty and that Parliament has decided to let the people decide by holding a referendum. Get the class to decide what question the referendum should ask and whether there should be more than one question. For example, as well as the question 'Are you in favour of reintroducing the death penalty?' there could be a second question asking 'Are you in favour of reintroducing the death penalty for particular crimes, namely the murder of police officers, treason and terrorist atrocities?

Divide the class into two groups – asking one group to prepare the arguments in favour and the other group to organise the arguments against. Then hold the debate before holding a secret ballot to decide whether they are for or against the reintroduction of the death penalty.

You could organise other similar debates on issues such as euthanasia and abortion. Alternatively, you could invite the children to research the gun laws in America and to debate the issue of whether the gun laws should be changed to abolish private citizens' rights to own guns.

CHAPTER 22

Environmental issues

This chapter contains activities on environmental issues such as the destruction of the rainforest, climate change, pollution, recycling and the growing of genetically modified crops. There are also activities which explore the environmental consequences of building a new reservoir and a new incinerator.

THE DESTRUCTION OF THE RAINFORESTS (Years 3–6 research/discussion)

Ask groups to draw a line down the middle of a large sheet of paper. On the left hand side of the paper ask them to write the heading 'Why the rainforest is disappearing'. On the right hand side of the paper ask them to write the heading 'Consequences of the rainforest disappearing'.

Use the poem 'Where is the forest?' to initiate a discussion of the reasons why the rainforest is disappearing. Elaborate on the reasons given in the poem and discuss how land is cleared for logging, for ranching and to build roads to provide access to mines in areas containing large deposits of valuable minerals such as copper.

Ask: What consequence of the destruction of the rainforest is mentioned in the poem? Encourage the children to use the internet to research other consequences of the destruction of the rainforest. Then compare their answers in a class discussion. Prompt them as necessary to discuss how plant species are being lost in addition to insect and animal species becoming extinct, how the destruction contributes to the greenhouse effect and how much of the land is left useless after the trees have been cut down because rain washes away the topsoil.

Where is the forest?

Where is the forest?
cried the animals.
Where are the trees?

We needed the wood,
said the people.
Wood to make fires.
Wood for our houses.
We cut it down.

Where is the forest?
cried the animals.
Where are the trees?

We needed the land,
said the people.
Land for out cattle.
Land for our roads.
We cut it down.

Where is the forest?
cried the animals.
Where is our home?

Gone, whispered the wind.
Gone. Gone. Gone.

HOW MUCH DO YOU KNOW ABOUT AIR POLLUTION?
(Years 3 and 4 quiz)

Aim: To increase pupils' knowledge of the causes and effects of air pollution.

Put the statements (below) on the board and ask the children individually to write down whether they are true or false, then to compare their answers in groups. Explain that all the statements are true. The reason children are more at risk is that they tend to spend more time than adults out of doors. Facts about air pollution can be found at the website www.eschooltoday.com

1. Every day you breathe in 20,000 litres of air.
2. Children are more at risk from air pollution than adults.
3. Motor vehicles produce more air pollution than any other human activity.
4. Four thousand people died in London in 1952 due to the smog produced by pollution.
5. Many districts in towns and cities are smokeless zones where you can only burn smokeless fuels.
6. Pollutants in the air can damage the lungs causing chest infections and diseases such as cancer and emphysema.
7. Chemicals released by factories can cause acid rain.
8. Acid rain can damage buildings and pollute the environment.
9. Industrial development in China has led to China having 15 of the 20 most polluted cities in the world.
10. In some cities the air quality is so bad that people sometimes have to wear face masks when they go out.

ATTITUDES TO AIR POLLUTION (Years 5 and 6 survey)

Aim: To investigate adults' attitudes towards air pollution.

Encourage the children to draw up a questionnaire to survey adults' attitudes towards air pollution. Ask groups to draft a list of questions to ask, before putting them on the computer and printing out the questionnaire. Prompt them to ask questions such as would you be prepared to use your car less often in order to reduce the amount of air pollution? Encourage them to ask people of different ages to complete the questionnaire to find out if younger people are more concerned about air pollution than older people.

When they have completed the survey, encourage them to analyse the results and ask: What did you learn from the survey about adults' attitudes to air pollution?

A CLEAN AIR CAMPAIGN (Years 7 and 8 contributing to a campaign)

Aim: To increase the children's awareness of air pollution issues.

Ask groups to imagine they have been asked to participate in a campaign to make people more aware of the causes and effects of air pollution. Encourage them to think of different ways of getting their message across and to prepare an item, such as a dramatic sketch, a leaflet or a set of posters aimed at either factory owners, car owners, local councillors or the general public.

GM FOODS (Years 7 and 8 discussion)

Use the poem below to initiate a discussion of the arguments for and against allowing the genetic modification of foods. Ask for a show of hands to indicate whether the children are for or against GM foods or simply not sure. Then encourage groups to use the internet to find out what arguments are used to support or oppose allowing GM foods to be produced. Hold a class debate of the issue, before asking for another show of hands. Ask children who have changed their minds to explain why.

Modified progress

They bred the seed. They fed the seed.
They nurtured it with care.
They promised a bumper harvest
For all the world to share.

They piled it high upon the shelves.
It glowed with health outside.
But who knows where the changes stop
When crops are modified?

SAVE THE PLANET (Years 5 and 6 card game)

Aim: To increase awareness of what individuals and families can do to help to stop climate change.

For this activity you need to ask groups to prepare a set of cards with these instructions on them – some in green ink, some in red.

Green cards	Red cards
You turn off lights.	You don't turn off lights.
You recycle everything you can.	You don't bother with recycling.
You compost waste.	You don't compost waste.
You reuse things like plastic bottles.	You throw away empty plastic bottles.
You reuse plastic bags.	You throw away plastic bags.
You walk or cycle short distances.	You go by car however far you're going.
You turn off electrical appliances.	You leave electrical appliances on stand-by.
You have solar panels.	You don't have solar panels.
You buy locally grown food.	You buy food that has travelled long distances.
You recycle garden waste.	You burn garden waste.
You refuse unwanted packaging.	You throw away cardboard and other packaging.
You use energy-saving light bulbs	You do not look at how much energy light bulbs use.
Your home has loft and wall insulation.	Your walls and loft have poor insulation.
Your windows are double-glazed.	Your windows are not double-glazed.
You have a car which uses petrol efficiently.	Your car is a gas guzzler.

In addition to the instruction cards, ask the children to make 40 blank cards. The game is for two or three people. To play ask the children to shuffle the instructions cards and to place them face down on the table. They then each take 10 of the blank cards and put the other blank cards on the table. They take it in turns to pick an instructions card. If they pick up a green card, they discard one of their blank cards. If they pick a red card, they pick up one of the blank cards. The object of the game is to get rid of as many of their blank cards as possible. The winner is the person who has the fewest blank cards at the end of the game.

After they have played the game, discuss what they have learned from it about the things individuals can do to help to cut down climate change.

THE VILLAGE (Years 7 and 8 role play)

Aim: To understand the issues that may arise when a new development is planned.

Ask the children to imagine that a nearby city Metrochester has expanded so quickly that it urgently needs to increase its water supply. The city council has, therefore, passed a resolution in favour of building a new reservoir. The reservoir will completely cover the village of Scotsby. Invite them to hold a public meeting at which people express their views on the proposal.

Ask the children to discuss who might attend such a meeting and what their attitude to the proposal would be and why. Their suggestions might include:

- The leader of Metrochester council, in favour of the scheme
- The leader of the Green party on Metrochester council, against the scheme
- The chair of Scotsby parish council, whose family have lived in the village for over 200 years
- A local farmer whose land will be flooded
- The owner of the village shop

- The owner of a construction company who would be involved in building the reservoir
- The residents of a local estate who would lose their homes.

Choose children to take on these specific roles and tell the remainder of the class to be members of the public. Then role play the meeting.

As a follow-up, individuals can write letters to the Metrochester Gazette expressing their views on the proposal.

THE INCINERATOR (Years 7 and 8 role play)

This is a similar activity to 'The village', but in this case the plans are to build a new incinerator on land near a village.

Ask the children to research all the reasons why people might be in favour of or against the proposed incinerator. Encourage them to find out why the campaigning organisation Friends of the Earth are opposed to the building of more incinerators and why local people might also be opposed to the idea. Ask: Who would be in favour of the proposal and why? Then ask them to suggest who might speak at a public meeting to discuss the proposal. Choose members of the class to role play the speakers and get the class to act out the public meeting.

As a follow-up you can invite the children to imagine they are members of SNOTTI (Say NO To The Incinerator) who are protesting against the proposal. Ask them in groups to draft a letter stating why they are against building the incinerator.

THE RECYCLING RAP (Years 3–6 poem for discussion)

Aim: To discuss the advantages of recycling.

Introduce the topic of recycling by reading and discussing the poem, then preparing a performance of it.

Discuss how much the school does to recycle things. Ask groups to decide how many stars on a 5-star scale they would give the school for its recycling and to give the reasons for their decisions.

The recycling rap

Listen to me children. Hear what I say.
We've got to start recycling. It's the only way
To save this planet for future generations –
The name of the game is reclamation.
You've got to start recycling. You know it makes sense.
You've got to start recycling. Stop sitting on the fence.
No more pussyfooting. No more claptrap.
Get yourself doing the recycling rap.

Come on and start recycling. Start today
By saving old newspapers, not throwing them away.
Don't just take them and dump them on the tip,
Tie them in a bundle and put them in the skip.

Get collecting, protecting the future's up to you.
Save all your old glass bottles and your jamjars too.
Take them to the bottle bank, then at the factory
The glass can be recycled, saving energy.

Don't chuck away that empty drink can.
Remember what I said. Start recycling, man.
Wash it, squash it, squeeze it flat and thin.
Take it to the Save-A-Can and post it in.

Listen to me children. Hear what I say.
We've got to start recycling. It's the only way
To save this planet for future generations -
The name of the game is reclamation.
You've got to start recycling. You know it makes sense.
You've got to start recycling. Stop sitting on the fence.
No more pussyfooting. No more claptrap.
Get yourself doing the recycling rap.

CHAPTER 23
Global issues

The activities in this chapter focus on global issues such as health and hunger. There are also activities focusing on refugees, the arms trade and nuclear weapons, plus a game designed to make children aware of the issue of having a clean water supply.

IF I RULED THE WORLD (Years 3 and 4 circle activity)

Aim: To make the children aware of global issues.

This is an introductory activity. Ask the children to think about one thing they would change in the world if they could. Then go round the circle asking them in turn to make a statement 'If I ruled the world I would...' explaining one thing that they would change. Make a list of the things they would like to change. Read out the list and ask them if there are any other things they would like to change. Either go round the circle again or ask individuals if there are any other things they would like to add to the list.

KEEPING HEALTHY (Years 5–6 a class assembly)

Aim: To understand what people need to keep healthy and that there are many people in the world who do not have these basic needs met.

Discuss with the class what things people need to keep them healthy. Draw up a list on the board: enough food to eat, clean water to drink, a clean environment, a safe environment, a proper sewage system, health care.

Explain that while we have all these things, there are many people in the world who do not.

Encourage them to use the internet to find out facts e.g. about how many people suffer from malnutrition in the world, how many people do not have a clean water supply, how many children die from diseases that could be prevented, how many families live in unsafe areas.

Invite them to prepare an assembly on what people need to keep healthy. They could divide the class into two groups The Healthy Haves and The Help-Us-Please Have-Nots. The Healthy Haves could explain in turn each of the things they have which enable them to stay healthy, then the Help-Us-Please Have-Nots explain that the conditions in which they live mean that they do not have these things. Selected members of the class could provide facts and figures in the form of Did you know... statements at appropriate points, such as: Did you know that malaria is the cause of over half a million deaths a year? Facts about malaria can be found at the World Health Organisation website www.WHO.int

WHAT ARE THE CAUSES OF HUNGER? (Years 7 and 8 discussion)

Aim: To discuss that there are so many people in the world suffering from malnutrition and hunger.

Put the list of suggested causes of world hunger on the board and ask groups to rank them in order starting with what they think is the main cause, then hold a class discussion in which you point out that poverty is the main cause, that overpopulation is not responsible, that there would be enough food for everyone if we used the land properly and that wars and natural disasters exacerbate the problem rather than cause it.

- Wars, which force people from their homes, cause starvation.
- Natural disasters such as drought and floods ruin crops.
- Poverty means people cannot buy food even if it is available.

- Land is used for growing crops such as cotton, tea, coffee and tobacco rather than food.
- Overpopulation means there is not enough food to feed everybody.
- Lack of education means people do not know how to make the best use of their land.
- Too much land is used for growing food for animals e.g. beef cattle rather than for crops which could feed humans.

THE ARMS TRADE (Years 7 and 8 discussion)

Aim: To debate whether Britain should stop manufacturing arms and selling them to other countries.

Market forces
(The arms dealer's defence)

We sold the guns
but we didn't know
where the guns
were going to go.

We didn't know.
Why should we care?
We needed to sell
the guns somewhere.

We sold the guns.
What's the fuss?
Someone wanted them.
Don't blame us!

Use the poem above to initiate a discussion of the arms trade. Ask: Should Britain stop manufacturing arms? What is meant by an ethical foreign policy? How can we stop arms from falling into the hands of dictators and terrorists?

Encourage them to discuss the idea that Britain should set an example and stop manufacturing arms. Ask groups to list arguments for and against this idea. Prompt them to consider the economic consequences of such a decision and the arguments of CAAT (the Campaign Against the Arms Trade) that by manufacturing and selling arms we are fuelling wars, wasting resources and supporting repressive regimes.

NUCLEAR WEAPONS (Years 7 and 8 debate)

Aim: To debate the issue of nuclear weapons.

Introduce the topic by asking for a show of hands to indicate whether or not they think nuclear weapons should be abolished. Then encourage groups to share their views on nuclear weapons by putting the statements (below) on the board. Ask them to draft speeches either for or against the motion 'This house believes that nuclear weapons should be abolished' and organise a debate, followed by a vote. Ask: Have any of you changed your minds after debating the issue? What made you change your minds?

- If nuclear weapons were abolished it would create world peace.
- Nuclear weapons are the main reason there hasn't been a World War 3.
- The consequences of a nuclear war would be so catastrophic for humanity that we should get rid of them.
- Abolition is not practical. Countries which have nuclear weapons would never agree to give them up.
- Abolishing nuclear weapons would remove the risk of them falling into the wrong hands.
- The money spent on maintaining nuclear weapons could be used for much better purposes.
- The world would be a much safer place without nuclear weapons.
- It's only the threat of nuclear strikes against it that keeps a country like North Korea from attacking its enemies.

REFUGEES (Years 5–8 discussion)

Aim: To think about what you would take with you if you suddenly became a refugee.

Present the children with this scenario. Imagine you are a government sympathiser in a country where there is civil war. You have been sent a threatening letter. You receive a message that opponents of the government are on their way to your house. You only have time to pick up to five things before you flee. What do you put in your rucksack?

Get the children in pairs to list the things they would take with them, then share their lists in a class discussion. Point out the importance of taking the threatening letter. They will need it if they are to apply for political asylum in another country, as proof that it is too dangerous for them to return to their native country.

Then ask them to imagine that they have several hours to prepare to flee, what else would they put in their rucksack? Imagine they have room for fifteen items. Invite them in a class discussion to compare their lists with Misra's list (below):

> passport, money, medicines, first aid kit, jewellery, water bottle, threatening letter, memory sticks, knife, matches, soap, socks, toilet paper, sweater, mobile phone.

LIFE AS A REFUGEE (Years 5–8 hotseating)

Aim: To understand what life is like for a refugee.

Invite groups of three to discuss what life would be like as a refugee. Prompt them to consider what living conditions would be like, how they would have only a tent for their family to share, how they would have to queue for food and water, how there would be no toys or gadgets to play with, how they would be separated from relatives and friends. Then encourage them to be hotseated as a refugee family – a father, a mother and a child.

THE WATER GAME (Years 5–8 board game)

Aim: To understand the problems that can lead to water shortages in certain less economically developed countries.

For this activity groups need to make a board on which to play the game and 12 water cards. Each group will also need counters and a dice.

First, they should make a board with 36 squares on it, consisting of a grid of six lines of six squares. The squares should be numbered 1 to 36 starting with the bottom left hand square. A W should be written on 12 of the squares e.g. 3, 6, 8, 10, 11, 17, 19, 24, 29, 30, 33, 34.

The 12 water cards need to have the following instructions written on them:

- The well on which you rely for water runs dry. Go back 10 spaces.
- A dam is built upstream from your village. The river which you rely on for irrigation is reduced to a trickle. Go back 8 spaces.
- The lake you rely on for water and fish is polluted. Go back 8 spaces.
- There has been no rain for 2 years. Go back 10 spaces
- Government plans to pipe water to your village are abandoned because of corruption. Go back 6 spaces.
- There is an outbreak of cholera caused by the lack of clean water. Go back 10 spaces.
- It rains heavily for a week. Go forward 6 spaces.
- A relief agency digs a new well. Go forward 8 spaces.
- The water pump breaks and it is months before supply to the village is restored. Go back 5 spaces.
- Members of your family have to walk 10 miles daily to fetch water. Miss a turn.
- Refugees from a nearby country arrive and there is not enough water for everyone. Miss 2 turns.
- The crops on which you depend shrivel and die from lack of water. Go back 8 spaces.

Explain that the object of the game is to overcome the difficulties that people experience in parts of the world due to lack of enough clean water and to reach square 36.

Before you begin, shuffle the cards and put them in a pile.

You take it in turns to throw the dice and to move your counter. Each time you land on a square with a W on it, you have to take a card and follow the instructions on it.

THE £5 MILLION CHALLENGE (Years 6–8 writing)

Aim: To consider which global issues are the most important.

Invite the children to imagine that a millionaire tycoon has said he will donate £5 million to an organisation which is committed to helping to solve a world problem. He has issued a challenge to young people to write a paragraph of not more than 150 words about a world problem saying they think he should donate the money to help solve that problem. Ask the children individually to write a paragraph about the issue that they think them money should be spent on. Brainstorm issues that they might focus on e.g. climate change, terrorism, world health, poverty, hunger, the arms trade, nuclear weapons, endangered species. The children can read their letters to the class and hold a vote to decide which letter presents the most convincing argument.

Get ready to...

Jumpstart!